D1085201

Advanced Praise for *Growth*

Nothing could prepare Karen DeBonis for the moment her eleven-year-old son, Matthew, was diagnosed with a brain tumor. *Growth: A Mother, Her Son, and the Brain Tumor They Survived* is a meditation on how we endure and heal throughout the struggles we encounter. Heartbreakingly painful and movingly inspiring, this memoir goes straight for your heart."

— Judy Goldman, author of *Child: A Memoir, a 2022 Katie Couric Media Must-Read New Book*

"In this engaging debut, Karen DeBonis describes the challenges of motherhood while navigating a frustrating and mysterious medical situation for her son. This is the perfect book for any mother who has searched for answers for a child or a greater understanding of herself."

— Julie Vick, author of *Babies Don't Make Small Talk (So Why Should I?): The Introvert's Guide to Surviving Parenthood*

"With honesty and awareness, DeBonis shares a journey not many of us can fathom. Beautiful storytelling pulled me into the author's and her son's journeys and held me captive. I'm a better person for having read this book."

— Ronni Robinson, author of *Out of the Pantry: A Disordered Eating Journey*

"DeBonis has written a raw, honest account of her son's medical condition both before and after his surgery and of her own fierce struggle to get him the help he needs from professionals who often refuse to take her fears seriously."

— Judy Barron, author of *There's a Boy in Here: Emerging from the Bonds of Autism*

"This book will resonate with anyone who has navigated--or is navigating--raising children with a long-term health condition, or who wants to be able to advocate effectively for themselves or their family. DeBonis illustrates again and again how listening to that quiet, inner voice we all have and actually trusting it, helps us summon the power to speak up and speak out when it matters."

—Helen Snape, award-winning Healthy Relationships Coach

"In language that ranges from pragmatic to poetic, suspenseful to insightful, Karen DeBonis invites you into her life as she evolves from a struggling, uncertain mother to a woman still facing trials but doing so with a new and stronger voice. This book holds universal truths for anyone who has been held back by the need to please others more than themselves."

— Judith Hannan, author of *Motherhood Exaggerated*

"Karen DeBonis's personal evolution is the compelling spine of a memoir that also walks a rapt reader through her son's convoluted diagnostic journey. *Growth* is a vulnerable and relatable glimpse into the heart of a mother who loses sight of the risks to herself when she is advocating for the child that she knows best."

— Patti M. Hall, author of *Loving Large: A Mother's Rare Disease Memoir*

"This brilliantly written book tells the struggle of a mother searching for answers while she watches her son's health deteriorate. The effort to overcome being a "people pleaser" to questioning professionals takes Karen DeBonis on a journey of growth. This is an excellent book for families who face numerous challenges--whether medical or educational--on the fight we all face to provide the best opportunities for our children."

— Lois Letchford, author of *Reversed: A Memoir*

"In her universe, DeBonis's peace-loving nature urges her to please everyone. In her reality, her maternal love will fully manifest only when she honors her own integrity. DeBonis's struggle and triumph illuminate the universal human effort to embrace one's true self. She writes with honesty and verve, her vulnerability and candor balanced by intelligence and wit. *Growth* is an exquisite offer. The reader emerges transformed."

— Allison Hong Merrill, author of *Ninety-Nine Fire Hoops*

"The name says it all. This is a book about growth in every direction and for everyone. This is a passionate, fast-moving and page-turning story about a mom who goes from the ultimate nice girl to a fierce fighter for her child. *Growth*: It's also a mystery story and a race against time—and the medical services system. This is a book for all of us for parents, educators, and child advocates. And for every woman who wants to be nice, until nice is just too dangerous."

— Diane Cameron, author of *Never Leave Your Dead: A History of Military Trauma*, and *Out of the Woods: A Woman's Journey to Long-term Recovery*

"Karen DeBonis's book instantly engaged me, as I identified with her journey. Her skillful writing proves itself with her clear-cut view into how her past affects her present. This book takes you on an authentic, heartfelt ride and had me smiling at the end."

— Ivy Tobin, author, actor, The Society for Recovering Doormats

GROWTH

*A Mother, Her Son, and the Brain
Tumor They Survived*

Karen DeBonis

Apprentice
House Press

Loyola University Maryland

First Edition

Library of Congress Control Number: 2022949905

Hardcover ISBN: 978-1-62720-434-7
Paperback ISBN: 978-1-62720-435-4
Ebook ISBN: 978-1-62720-436-1

Design by Claire Marino
Editorial Development by Sophie LaBella

Published by Apprentice House Press

Loyola University Maryland
4501 N. Charles Street, Baltimore, MD 21210
410.617.5265
www.ApprenticeHouse.com
info@ApprenticeHouse.com

To Matt. Without you, I don't know who I would have been, but I don't think I would have liked that woman much. Your presence in my life allowed me to discover my best self. What a gift.

"If you're acting like a sheep, do not blame the shepherd."
—Papaji (Sri H.W.L. Poonja)

Contents

Author's Note

Writing this memoir was sometimes a battle of fact vs. memory. Fact—when verifiable—always won. In the absence of documentation, I portrayed what I remembered to the best of my ability. As author Mary Karr once said, "Memoir shows lived experience, not surface reporting."

I did change names and identifying details of key characters because, of course, they are real people—human and fallible like the rest of us--and I have no desire to drag anyone through the mud of poor decisions.

Content warning:
Post-partum depression, eating disorders, suicidal gestures.

Part 1

1

A Reckoning

I first noticed Matthew's eye-rolling the summer he turned eight. It wasn't the typical "Mom, quit bugging me" look. It was more like an ocular Ferris wheel, brown eyes circling around and around, taking in the view, enjoying the thrill. Up. Right. Down. Left. Up right down left. Uprightdownleft, several times, until it came to rest as if to take on new riders. Then the ride started up again.

Sprawled on the living room carpet, Matthew was oblivious to me watching from the kitchen. He hand-surfed through a pile of Legos, making a ruckus of *clickety-clicks*. The funny cowlick that defied hair gel and spit protruded from his crown, and his *Goosebumps* T-shirt grew a soggy ring at the neckline where he chewed and sucked on it in concentration.

"There it is!" he proclaimed, his eyes taking a joyride as he held aloft a tiny yellow helmet.

Bringing attention to a child's troublesome behavior often

exacerbates it, so I said nothing. But I registered eye-rolling in the part of my brain where back-to-school paperwork, grocery lists, and work deadlines already overflowed. I could hardly imagine adding to my mother-load, but I filed Matthew's unusual behavior under H for "Hmmm," dated August 1994. Then I turned to the fridge to figure out what to fix for dinner.

Nearly thirty-six, I thought I had my working mom act together—two kids, one husband, an old house, and a hyperactive border collie mutt. But some days, I looked at the calendar and thought, *I just have to get through this week, then I can breathe.* Sometimes I "just" had to get through the month until I could breathe, and I wondered if I'd remember how.

That evening, Matthew played in the backyard with Stephen, three, and Sparky, our adopted dog. Mike, my husband of twelve years, sat on a kitchen chair in shorts and a ratty T-shirt, lacing up his work boots.

"Did you notice Matthew's eye-rolling during dinner?" I asked.

"Yeah, I did." He didn't look up, and I stared at a tuft of his thick, brown hair sticking out from the back of his New York Yankees hat.

"I think it's a tic," I said.

"What does that mean?" He glanced at me curiously.

"I don't know." I twisted my hair in a knot, then let it fall, unsure of what I wanted to say. "It's probably not a big deal, but I'll mention it when Matthew has his physical."

"Good idea." He stood and gave me a quick peck on the cheek. "I'd better get out in that garage before it gets dark."

Mike easily put the conversation aside. Not one to overthink or analyze things, he returned to what he knew—that our ramshackle garage was falling down, that it might be salvaged with cables and braces and his architect's ingenuity. A tic was an oddity he didn't understand and couldn't fix. He easily pushed it into a corner of his mind like our Christmas decorations in the attic, forgotten until I asked him to drag them out again.

At Matthew's annual well-child visit the following week, he sat on the padded table in his underwear, still too young to be bashful. Swinging his legs, he alternated butt cheeks in time to an invisible marching band. Giggling at his inventiveness, he crooked his arms and swung along.

I smiled, shaking my head. "Silly goose."

As soon as the doorknob clicked, Matthew stopped all but the leg-swinging. He always wanted to behave, especially in public.

"Third grade already, Matthew?" Dr. Peterson exclaimed, bursting through the door. "You're getting to be so grown up!"

When Mike and I were expecting in 1986, we weren't savvy enough to interview prospective pediatricians like parents often do today, and it probably wasn't an option anyway. Our health plan, a local, fledgling HMO (Health Maintenance Organization), limited their coverage to a finite group of in-network doctors. They had one pediatrician on staff, so that's who we got.

We got lucky. Around ten years my senior, Dr. Peterson had a friendly face with a big smile full of big teeth. A mother of three older children, she had doctored hundreds of babies.

More importantly, she never condescended to us due to our inexperience. Whatever the ailment or concern, she educated us in terms we understood without being patronizing.

Matthew politely answered her casual inquiries about his summer, his friends, the upcoming school year. When she finished, Dr. Peterson gave him a canister of *Star Wars* stickers to choose from and turned to me.

"Any new concerns in the family?"

"Did you notice his eyes?" I whispered from behind my hand while Matthew dug in the jar.

She stared at Matthew for a minute.

"Matthew," she said, "are your eyes bothering you?"

"Uh-uh." He shook his head back and forth vigorously.

"Are they itchy?"

"No."

"When I was a little girl," she said, "I rolled my eyes when they felt itchy."

I knew that wasn't the problem, but she continued in a friendly, matter-of-fact tone.

"You can stop it, can't you, Matthew?"

Don't you know any *child psychology? You can't ask a kid a leading question and expect an honest answer.*

For ten seconds, while Dr. Peterson counted, Matthew stopped eye-rolling. As soon as she finished, his eyes made up for lost time.

Doesn't that tell you something?

But my face revealed none of my annoyance, my smile plastered in place. When the doctor concluded that Matthew had a "habit tic"—a growing pain he'd outgrow—impotent words dribbled from my mouth. "Oh, good," and "That's great," two of my go-to responses for just about everything. And of course, "Thank you," not only to be polite, but to stay in the good graces of a person I liked, in hopes she'd like me back, which was everything.

When I was six, my mother brought me to her hair salon for a trim of my long, thick hair. The petite hairdresser with a tall pile of bleached curls took an inch or two off my length, then, brandishing her thinning shears, left billowing piles of blond fluff on the floor and a pencil-thin ponytail on my head. I felt as light as a butterfly. When we got home, I flitted around for my dad, showing off my skinny hair. My mom waited for me to flutter away before she said anything to my dad, but she didn't wait long enough.

"All Karen's beautiful hair," I heard her whisper. "It's ruined."

I didn't understand. Mommy sounded mad, but I saw her smile at the lady and tell her my haircut looked nice. I thought they were friends. Mommy said, "Thank you." Mommy was so nice, she would never really be mad at someone.

At six years old, I had learned some important rules:

1. When you're mad, act like you're not, at least until you get home.
2. Be nice, even if you don't mean it.
3. Always be agreeable, even if your hair is ruined.

2

I'm Fine

One evening when I was twelve, my parents went out with friends, leaving me in charge of my four younger siblings in our five-bedroom raised ranch in the suburbs of Pittsburgh. I don't know why my parents didn't ask my thirteen-year-old brother Brian to babysit. Maybe he didn't like doing it. Or maybe they asked me because I liked the responsibility. Or maybe because, in 1970, babysitting was considered a girl's job. My parents were progressive in many ways—my dad changed diapers and my mom easily wielded a screwdriver and hammer—but otherwise, our family conformed to most traditional gender roles.

After my parents drove away, I sat on the couch in the family room with my younger siblings. Mary Beth, eight, and John, four, cuddled close to me as I read them a book. Paul, ten, too old and already too prickly to cuddle, hunched over a bowl of Cheerios in the adjacent harvest-gold kitchen, listening. Mark, the baby, sat on my lap, helping to turn pages. When it was his bedtime, I rocked him to sleep with a bottle, singing *Puff the Magic Dragon.*

My parents wouldn't have gone out that night if they knew one of us was sick to the point of throwing up, but one of us was, and Mary Beth did. After I got the younger boys settled for the night, my sister curled up in my parents' bed with the lights out. Across the hall in the bedroom she and I shared, I sat on my twin bed, flipping through *Teen* magazine ogling pictures of Davy Jones, the cutest of the Monkees.

Mary Beth appeared at the bedroom door, her brown hair disheveled, her face pale.

"I threw up in the bathroom."

"Okay, go back and lie down. I'll take care of it."

In the tiny bathroom off my parents' bedroom, the sink—not the toilet—brimmed with a putrid slurry. I loved to nurture, but Mary Beth was my sister after all, so I yelled at her for throwing up in the sink, which was now clogged. I dunked my bare arm through what felt like soupy oatmeal to pull up the stopper, gagging as my nails filled with slime. But I got the job done.

What I accomplished that night felt like a badge of honor. It meant I had what it took to be a mom. When I did become a mother years later, if all that had been required was to be loving and nurturing and able to deal with the occasional explosion of bodily fluids, I would have been fine. But my resume full of experience had not prepared me for Matthew.

Two days after my due date in August 1986, I lay on the exam table, maternity dress hiked above my bump, underwear pushed below. A petite obstetrician measured my belly. *Did she just make a face?* She measured again, furrowing her brow.

"Have you had any leaking?"

"No, not that I've noticed."

"Hmm." She looked at my belly again. "You are rather small."

Was she asking if my water had broken? It hadn't, and my armpits moistened as my mind raced. I had given up alcohol, caffeine, painting my nails, and highlighting my hair. I had taken my vitamins. How could something be wrong when I had done everything right?

Within the hour, Mike met me at the hospital, and we had barely enough time for a hug before rushing to radiology for an emergency ultrasound. It revealed a dangerously low level of amniotic fluid, a condition called *oligohydramnios*. A physician or radiologist must have conveyed the information, but I have no recollection of an actual person speaking. I remember only key words—uncommon, dangerous, risk, birth defects—and the fearful looks Mike and I shared.

I spent the next week in the high-risk maternity ward. My roommate was a sweet woman about my age—twenty-seven—also admitted toward the end of her pregnancy. Mike and I became friendly with her and her husband. By my second or third day, it became clear she was having a miscarriage, and her husband pulled the curtains around their gloom. I was all too aware of what was happening, all too aware it could happen to me. Then, hearing sobs from behind the curtain, Mike quickly pulled me into the hall and into his arms, where I cried.

A passing nurse stopped and gently laid her hand on my

shoulder.

"Would you like us to put you in a different room?" She nodded her head in presumption of a "yes."

She asked the wrong question. Or rather, *asking* was the wrong tactic. Had she told me I was being moved, I would have been grateful. Had she made the decision, I would have complied. But I didn't want to inconvenience the nursing staff; they were so busy, after all. And I didn't want my roomie to feel bad for driving me away.

I managed a weak smile and shook my head.

"No. I'm fine."

Mike and I roamed the halls for a while before peeking back into my room. The woman and her husband were gone, as was, presumably, their baby.

Finally, my doctors decided to induce labor, and on August 13, 1986, we became a family.

"It's a boy!" a nurse cried.

"It's a boy!" I screamed, drumming my feet in the stirrups.

A bevy of neonatologists whisked away our high-risk boy. Thankfully, none of the oligohydramnios scares had been realized, and the specialists quickly gave our five-pound, eleven-ounce son the all-clear. Small for a full-term baby, his APGAR was nonetheless perfect, and I took credit. What an exemplary mother I was already. Just look at my perfect child!

When at last I held our newborn in my arms, Mike and I took one look and whispered reverently, "Matthew." His dark eyes blinked at me. I felt I had known him forever, and we locked gazes, our souls embracing like long-lost friends. "Matthew, it's me," I cooed. "It's Mommy." He frowned and his chin trembled, wrinkling like a raisin. I caressed his cheek, knowing that throughout this child's life, I'd do anything to soothe his sorrows.

Near midnight, our threesome arrived in my darkened room where two other new moms slept quietly in their corners. After Mike left, Matthew started to cry, mewing softly like a kitten. I tried to get his tiny mouth to latch onto my huge nipple, but despite breastfeeding classes and my mother's example, having breastfed all six of her children, I clearly lacked the skill. Matthew's face turned red with exertion, and the mewing became bleating, then bawling as I labored for twenty minutes to get him attached.

When I finally succeeded, I let him nurse for five minutes as I had learned, then gently eased my finger into his mouth to break the suction. The noisy battle continued on the other side until, after another twenty minutes, Matthew got a grip. I glanced nervously at the two other beds. *They must hate me.*

For the rest of the night, every hour, it seemed, Matthew and I performed our dance of intimacy:

Twenty minutes of crying, five minutes of nursing, switch.

Twenty minutes of crying, five minutes of nursing, stop.

If the breastfeeding instructor had warned of these difficulties, I must have tuned out, doubting the information's relevance to me. And I'm sure my mother never complained about nursing being hard. The problem, I assumed, lay within me. I was supposed to be a natural. What happened?

Mike showed up late the next morning because he had other priorities. Six weeks before my due date, a week before closing on our first house, the bank approved our mortgage application with a contingency: the electrical service had to be brought up to code within three months. Hiring a contractor cost a small fortune, so days after we moved in, Mike knocked holes in the walls and began rewiring every light fixture, switch, and outlet in the 1920's three-bedroom, one-bath Dutch colonial.

Most pregnant women couldn't wait to deliver by their ninth month. Not me. Our home was no place for a baby. If Sweetpea wanted to hang out in my womb a while longer, it was fine with me.

When Mike finally arrived at the hospital, we *oohed* and *aahed* for a couple of hours over our beautiful baby. Then I shooed him away. There was nothing I needed from him there, while at home he had a maze of wires and Swiss-cheese walls to tackle. The nursery still had no power, and the electricity wouldn't finish itself. "I'll be fine," I told him. *I'll be fine,* I told myself.

After he left, I rolled over and sobbed into the pillow. But we were adults now; my emotional needs paled in comparison to practical concerns like functioning electrical outlets. A mom had to place the welfare of her children and her family above her own. It was part of the sleepless nights, spit-up, poopy diapers scenario for which I'd mentally prepared.

The day of our closing, Mike decided to rent a carpet shampooer because he worried about the baby crawling around on the shag wall-to-wall in the living and dining rooms. After the stress and excitement of signing a thirty-year mortgage, I pined for the couch in our old apartment where I could put my feet up and blast the air conditioner. But I waddled along with Mike for "moral support," as he called it. We didn't think to bring a chair or cushion, so I eased myself down on the floor in the corner near the kitchen and watched Mike push and pull the bulky machine across the rooms. "It looks good, dear," I said, thinking to myself, *I don't give a damn how it looks*.

On moving day, during a record-breaking heatwave, I felt every one of the forty-plus pounds I'd gained in pregnancy. I directed friends and the incoming boxes until the U-Haul was empty and our home looked like a warehouse. One couple hung on after the others had left, but it felt rude to excuse myself and lie down. I stayed in the kitchen, offering beers, making small talk, lusting for the cool white sheets in my newly made bed upstairs.

Couldn't they see I was exhausted? Couldn't Mike? Why didn't someone give me an opening to leave? *Karen, you must be tired. You should rest.* But without explicit permission to take care of my needs, I remained, barefoot and pregnant in the kitchen.

Before work a few days later, Mike opened the fridge to inspect its contents.

"Karen, can you get some chicken started on the hibachi after you get home from work?"

"Sure." At the moment, I meant it. Mike longed to cook out on our tiny deck, and I hated to disappoint him. Plus, I got home a good hour before him. If we waited for Mike to start dinner, I'd starve.

"It'll be so great," Mike said. "Just think. Our own deck!"

I arrived home from work drugged with fatigue. But I lit the coals, rinsed the chicken, and got it sizzling. Then I collapsed in a low-slung lawn chair, our only outdoor seating. To get out of it, I had to pull on the deck railing to heave myself up, peeling my sweaty thighs from the vinyl strips. When Mike got home, dinner was cooked, and I was fried.

It never occurred to Mike that I should rest, and it never occurred to me to tell him. Since I never told him about my needs, he had no way of knowing what they were. In fact, he may not have realized I had needs at all.

By the time we came home after two nights in the hospital, the nursery's lights and electrical outlets worked, and its surfaces shone, thanks to Mike. He carried Matthew upstairs and gently placed him in his new white crib. I closed the pastel curtains I'd sewn, trying to block the afternoon sun. Mike and I held hands, shoulder to shoulder, looking down at Matthew's thin legs, his arms drawn in tight. How apropos that I'd dressed him in a sailor onesie—he practically swam in it.

I tried to sense that heart-throbbing, all-consuming love I'd read about, but it wasn't there. Yes, I felt amazed and in awe of this child we'd created. Yes, I loved him. But I couldn't summon the deep feelings I'd expected. It felt like needing a good cry but not being able to start the tears.

Mike kissed me and left to go downstairs. I wanted to unpack, but Matthew's twitches, wheezes, and whimpers kept me glued in place. In all the years I babysat as a teen, I had little experience with newborns. Even with four younger siblings, I never realized these tiniest of tots were so restless. Or maybe they weren't—not like Matthew. As an adult, I'd heard other mothers say they could spend hours watching their babies sleep, but every grunt made me uneasy.

My mom wasn't an obsessive worrier. I suppose with six kids, the many immediate needs left her little mental energy to expend on what-ifs. But I had a college friend whose mother wouldn't let him drive back to town the summer after graduation. Apparently, she worried he'd have an accident. I didn't get it at the time.

But six years later, as I hovered over my own flesh-and-blood, I got it. At that very moment, with Matthew propped on his side between the crib pads and a rolled-up baby blanket—the recommended SIDS-prevention position at the time—I became a worrier. The awesome responsibility of motherhood and all its potential disasters hit. I worried if I left the room, Matthew would stop breathing. I worried he'd choke. When he started walking, he'd fall down the stairs, when he got his first bike, he'd fly over the handlebars, when he drove, he'd fall asleep behind the wheel. Finally, I tore myself away to unpack, but every few minutes, I peeked in to make sure Matthew was still breathing.

In those early days, I rarely fed Matthew in bed at night so as not to disturb Mike. My siblings had chipped in on a rocking chair for us, but it hadn't yet arrived. Until then, I perched on a wooden folding chair with no support for my arms or feet. I could have gone downstairs to nurse, but I was too tired and too complacent to bother.

When my mom flew in from Pittsburgh a few days later and saw my awkward nursing set-up, she suggested carrying up one of the living room chairs. I pictured her and Mike dragging the swiveling, upholstered beast stair-by-stair to the nursery. I didn't want them to go to all that trouble.

"I'm fine," I assured her.

Had Mom insisted I get a comfortable chair or ordered me to take a nap or seized the baby so I could shower, I would have agreed. But my mother was agreeable, too. She wasn't one to impose her advice on anyone, including her daughter.

3

Learned Agreeableness

A few years before I had Matthew, my mom and I attended the bridal shower of a family friend in Pittsburgh. On the way back to my parents' house, Mom rolled her window down, the oppressive August air ruffling her short, permed hair. Over the drone of traffic, we chatted about the guests, the gifts, the fiancé who stopped in at the end. I hadn't met him before, but Mom had. He appeared to be a big, friendly guy with no fashion sense whatsoever, wearing baggy black pants, clunky black shoes, and thick white socks.

"It's too bad he wears those ugly socks," Mom said, checking her rearview mirror.

I whipped my head in her direction. I had never heard my mother make an even remotely derogatory comment about another individual. In fact, the more glaringly obvious a person's flaws, the more Mom exaggerated or invented a compliment. If she truly disliked an acquaintance, I might detect a negative vibe, but it remained subtle and unspoken. And to pass judgment on a person's attire? Unthinkable. Clothing was superficial, not indicative of character.

"What did you say?" I asked, laughing.

"I just think his socks are a little out of style, that's all."

She didn't take her eyes from the road, and I couldn't read her expression. Did she not understand the enormity of her words?

I blurted out the first, ineloquent thing that came to mind.

"See, Mom, you can do that. You can say something a little negative about someone and it doesn't mean you're judging them." I kept my tone light, carefree, a bit of fun between girlfriends. I took care not to offend her.

If she replied, I don't remember, my mind a thunderstorm of confusion.

That evening, I lay in the spare bed in the house where I grew up, mulling over my earlier conversation. I understood why a mother would carefully screen her comments around her youngsters. You never know what your kid might repeat at an inopportune time and place. I also knew and appreciated my parents' intention to imbue their children with Catholic values they held dear—that all people are children of God, regardless of skin or shoe or sock color. That what you wear or drive or how you look is not a statement of your character. That you must love thine enemy. Turn the other cheek. Forgive. And of course, always be agreeable.

I fluffed my pillow and rolled on my back. *If Mom, who has such moral integrity, can pass judgment on a person's socks, what does that mean for me?*

During another Pittsburgh visit in my twenties, my parents and I sat around the huge kitchen table my dad had built years earlier to accommodate our family of eight. Church bulletins, coupons, and grocery lists crammed the giant bulletin board on the wall. The avocado refrigerator hummed in the background. We relaxed with a glass of wine after a short visit from some former neighbors for whom I used to babysit. The soft-spoken mother had always engaged me in pleasantries. The opinionated and obnoxious father made me uncomfortable, not that I ever told anyone.

We came to a pause in the conversation and Dad broke the silence.

"I always thought that guy was a bit of a louse."

As he announced his verdict, he stared down at my mom and then me as if daring us to disagree.

I squirmed. Suddenly, I was nine again, fearing my father's biting criticism. He frequently professed "I love you," and demonstrated it through Saturday morning pancake feasts, a homemade skating rink in our backyard, and family excursions to the public pool. But my father didn't tolerate being questioned by his children. Dad befriended homeless people, rescued stranded motorists, played catch with the neighborhood children, but at home, his quick temper taught me to keep my mouth shut.

My mother broke the tension, dispelling the words of disparagement hovering in the air. "Now Don, our neighbor had some wonderful qualities." Then she rambled about the necklace the neighbor bought his wife and the time he helped a friend carry a ladder.

Like my mother's ugly sock comment, my father's "louse" declaration was an anomaly. Later that night, I turned my dad's words over and over in my mind like a rotisserie. His comment was so out of character, I had no idea what to make of it.

Growing up, Mike learned to speak up to defend his domain because DeBonis Grocery, his family's livelihood, depended on it. If a bigger, tougher kid tried to sneak out the door with a bag of potato chips behind his back, Mike didn't hesitate to stop him. "Put it back," he'd command. So simple. My mom would have looked the other way, pretending not to see the offense rather than confronting the individual. My dad would have quipped, "It's only a bag of chips. He probably needs them more than I do." I might have done both.

I met Mike through mutual friends our senior year at Catholic University in Washington, D.C. He was a nice guy and easy to talk to, but I was seeing another senior at the time and had no romantic interest in someone new.

When several plastic cups of cheap wine at a campus party emboldened me to tell off the other guy, I latched on to Mike. We danced for the rest of the night, and he walked me home. Through the haze of intoxication, I became aware of his lips sloppily locked with mine, and before my mind could process what had happened, we unlocked long enough to agree to meet the following evening at the dining hall. The next morning, I woke with a hangover and regrets. I didn't even *like* Mike, not in the boyfriend way. But I had made a promise, so I met him for dinner, prepared to tell him it was all a drunken mistake.

Mike was waiting outside the dining hall when I walked up. Moving through the line, we made awkward conversation, then we settled across from each other in the red vinyl booth closest to the salad bar. Busy students and staff scurried back and forth, balancing speckled trays laden with cups of coffee, seconds of apple crisp, Sunday night mystery meat.

"This is kind of embarrassing," I said, "but I don't know your last name.

"Phew! I don't know yours either."

Laughing, we shared our names, neither of which were easily decipherable in the noisy hall, so we pulled out our driver's licenses.

"Rampolla," he read. "Is that Italian?"

"Yes. I'm also Irish and a little German. And DeBonis—is that French?"

He laughed. "No—Italian. Full blooded. And it's not 'dee-BONE-is.' It's 'duh-BAH-nis' like, I dunno, "honest.""

I held off talking about our entanglement the previous evening. As we got to know each other, I shyly took in his dark-chocolate eyes and wavy hair, his outdated shirt. I went gaga. That's how I've always described it: "gaga" as in I couldn't think about anything except how sexy his hairy forearm was. He wasn't some macho jock or poly-sci blowhard or stuck-up prep. He was sincere and kind and polite and respectful—the nicest guy I had ever met. I had found a keeper.

We started seeing each other regularly, and one night, at a big school party, a guy I recognized from campus came on to me. In the crush of the crowd, his hand brushed my breast. I wasn't sure it was intentional, but when I told Mike and pointed out the offender, Mike charged him, warning, "Stay the hell away from my girlfriend."

I was flattered, but being defended felt unfamiliar, and the conflict made me uncomfortable. We didn't do things that way in my family.

As a kid, I saw a story on TV about a home invasion.

"Dad, if a man came into our house and tried to attack us, would you fight him?"

I wanted my father to say, "I'd do anything to protect my family." Or, "I'd kill him if I had to." Instead, he mumbled about peace and non-violence and God's children.

Within the four walls of my childhood home, I felt safe. But out in the world, I knew I was on my own—loved and supported, but unprotected. I knew Mike would fill that void.

With dreams of becoming a child psychologist, I majored in psychology. Mike majored in architecture, and we graduated together in May 1980. We roomed with friends in separate houses close to each other in the D.C. suburbs and married two years later. The following spring, Mike's position as drafts-man was cut, and we talked about leaving D.C. for a more bud-get-friendly place to raise a family. When he received an offer near Troy, his hometown in upstate New York, we bade fare-well to big city life and packed a U-Haul, excited for the prom-ise of the future.

4

Boundaries

We first met Dr. Peterson at Matthew's one-week checkup. A Mickey Mouse stethoscope around her neck, she clapped her hands in delight and exclaimed, "So, this is Matthew!" Then she extended her hand to us.

"Nice to meet you, Mr. and Mrs. DeBonis. How is new parenthood?"

"Great!" I said. It felt like the polite response while we got acquainted.

In reality, Matthew still had trouble breastfeeding and took only a few ten-minute naps during the day. In between, he didn't resemble the cherubic, peaceful babies like those gracing the cover of *Parents* magazine. He fretted and squirmed constantly, it seemed. Then, by 4 p.m., he started wailing, and it didn't stop for five or six hours, no matter how much swaddling, tummy rubbing, singing, or walking Mike and I did. After the worst of it wore off, Matthew continued to fuss until one or two in the morning, when he finally settled down, and I crashed until the next feeding in an hour.

What happened to newborns who supposedly slept twenty hours a day, according to all the baby books I'd read? I had access to stacks of best sellers in the Russell Sage College library where I worked, "interlibrary loan clerk" being the only decent job I'd found since we'd moved to Troy. Free tuition offset the terrible pay, so at night, I took classes toward a master's degree in community health education. On my lunch breaks, if I wasn't studying smoking-related mortality rates or the health risks of processed foods, I pored over the wisdom of Dr. T. Berry Brazelton, Dr. Benjamin Spock, and any other experts I could find. Those baby books became my bibles.

After Dr. Peterson clucked and fussed like a mother hen over our "tiny baby," she began her exam. Although I relished the quiet of Matthew's mid-morning peaceful spell, I regretted the pediatrician wouldn't witness my child's full wrath.

Mike and I then spilled our tale of woe and Dr. Peterson listened carefully to our concerns. "Your baby is perfectly healthy, and his crying is to be expected. It's colic, which he'll outgrow."

The baby bibles advised that colic could take six months to outgrow. *Matthew will practically be driving by then.* Still, Mike and I felt enormous relief, grateful to have a physician we trusted who seemed to return the sentiment. And she liked me, I was sure.

Before we had kids, Mike and I talked about parenting duties. I made it clear he would do his share of diaper changing and bottle feeding, as well as laundry, dishes, and cleaning. Two working parents should divide the chores fifty-fifty. Although the idea of wiping poop from a baby's bottom initially freaked him out, Mike agreed. I was proud of my husband for being progressive. In his world growing up, men didn't change diapers.

One night, he tackled a particularly nasty diaper while I stood nearby handing him baby wipes and wet washcloths. I didn't want him to have to deal with the mess on his own. Not a breastfed newborn explosion like Matthew's.

After our joint cleanup, I said, "I'll give Mr. Poopyface a bath if you switch the laundry in the basement."

"Sure."

"And if you bring up the clean clothes, I'll fold them while we watch TV."

"No problem."

A dozen chores needed attention, and Mike would have done any one of them had I asked. But I had to ask. And I hated to ask. I felt like a nag. Often, it was easier to do it myself.

Matthew was almost two weeks old the first time we brought him to Mass at 8 a.m. I preferred to go later, but we'd always attended the early celebration with Mike's parents and brother. I needed a big head start, so when my alarm went off at five, I jumped out of bed. Mike had to get himself up for work five days a week. When he had a chance to sleep in, I made sure he did.

I tiptoed downstairs and nestled into the soft cushions of the living room couch. Outside, the day was still dark, the birds singing their morning chorus. I rested for a few minutes, willing my breathing to slow, my body to relax, my milk to flow. I needed to express enough for our outing, then give my body time to replenish its supply for Matthew's morning feeding. Using my plastic handheld breast pump, I eventually squeezed out a few ounces to hold us over.

Nursing discreetly in the back of church or in the car might have worked for other women, but not for me. I had always been ashamed of my big, pendulous breasts. Chubby as a kid, I slimmed down when my height shot up in early puberty. As a teen, I packed on weight again, carrying the excess fat in my belly and breasts. I had never undressed in front of girlfriends or my college roommates. I turned my back to undress in front of Mike. During pregnancy, my mammary glands enlarged like rising bread dough. Our Lamaze instructor said most women tear off their clothes during labor, preferring to be completely unencumbered. I kept my nursing bra on the whole time. And now, to get my lactating girls back in their cups, I practically needed a crane. It was not a feat I'd attempt in public.

When I finished pumping on the couch, I tiptoed back upstairs and dressed silently. By then, it was 6:30. I woke Matthew, changed, fed, re-changed, and dressed him. Mike's alarm went off, and at 7:30, he ran down the stairs fully clothed.

"C'mon, we have to go." He tossed his car keys from hand to hand as I scurried to heat the spare bottle and pack the diaper bag. I strapped Matthew in the portable car seat and Mike picked him up. "Anything I should do to help?" he asked.

"No, I got it."

Slinging the diaper bag over my shoulder, I followed Mike out the door. I needed to use the bathroom but that would make us late.

Later that week, I suggested that on Saturday we hang curtains and finish unpacking. Mike agreed. On Saturday morning, he sat at the kitchen counter with his coffee, scooping Wheaties into a bowl.

"Today, I'm going to finish that light switch in the hallway." He held up one finger, then two more. "Then I have to figure out why the lawnmower won't start, and if there's time, I'll clear that brush over by the fence."

I'd been up for two hours with Matthew and stood in the doorway, swaying back and forth with him. The sun beat in through the filthy windows, highlighting a cobweb in the corner of the room.

"That would be great to get that switch working," I said, without mentioning our agreement. After all, light was a necessity, we needed a working lawn mower, and the brush was unsightly. I made an objective assessment of priorities and decided Mike's to-do list mattered more than mine. I considered it a strength to be reasonable and practical, to willingly push my needs aside.

While Mike tackled his chores, I nursed, changed, entertained, and comforted Matthew, washed and folded two loads of laundry, and fixed spaghetti and garlic bread for dinner. I felt like I had done nothing of significance, so why was I exhausted?

After dinner, Mike wiped his mouth and got up from the table.

"Is it okay if I leave my dish here?"

"Sure. You go relax. I'll take care of cleaning up." He had worked so hard, after all.

A few days later, I stumbled into the kitchen one morning just before Mike left for work. He kissed me, then stepped back.

"Bad night?"

"Yeah. I was up with him five times. But he's sleeping now."

Mike pulled me in for a hug. "I wish he didn't keep you up so much. I'm lonely in the morning."

My heart melted and I snuggled tighter against him. Having read all about men who felt jealous of their new baby, I vowed my husband would not be one of them. Beginning the next morning, I got up with Mike's alarm and visited with him until he left for work. Then, too awake to go back to sleep, I puttered around the house. A few hours later, Matthew woke for the day, and I was already spent.

By the time I heard Mike's car pull up that evening, I had been pacing the floor with a screeching baby for what felt like days. "Daddy's home," I cooed to Matthew as I watched Mike through the front door window. He got out of his car and gathered his briefcase and jacket from the back seat. Looking down at a rear tire, he kicked it, then locked the doors and waved to a neighbor. Halfway up the sidewalk steps, he stopped and stared at the house, watching the paint dry, or so it seemed. Apparently, he didn't see his frantic wife and screaming baby through the window. Or maybe he did.

Mike finally stepped inside, took one look at us, and scoffed,

"What's wrong with *him*?"

I gulped back a gasp and tightened my hold on Matthew. *What a horrible thing to say about your own son.*

Mike's snarky tone only snuck out when he didn't understand something or was caught off guard. Despite wanting to yell at him, I rationalized on his behalf. He didn't mean to be cruel. He doesn't understand babies. I need to help him learn. It never occurred to me that confronting Mike about his insensitive comment would teach him more about being a good father than all the forgiveness I could muster. I never considered what confronting him might teach *me*.

"He's a baby," I responded calmly. "This is what babies do. They cry." Although inside, I wasn't convinced any baby cried like Matthew.

The look on my face must have given me away. Mike instantly softened, gently touching my arm.

"What's wrong?"

"Just a long day." I wiped my eyes and accepted his kiss, then he took Matthew and nuzzled his red face.

"Did you give Mommy a hard time today?"

I smiled at Mike's tenderness before rushing to the kitchen to start dinner. Dumping a screaming baby on my overworked husband filled me with guilt. I wanted to fix him something delicious tonight.

5

Secrets

After Mike left for work each day, the long, unstructured hours ahead stretched before me. *Now what?* Tending to Matthew was demanding, boring, and tedious. I loved to sleep in and enjoyed a good nap, but during my waking hours, I liked to be productive. Yet I lacked the energy to unpack the moving boxes still stacked in corners. I felt guilty wasting time on daytime TV, and Matthew distracted me too much to read. To express milk, pack the diaper bag, and venture out with a baby on my own sounded intimidating and exhausting. Home became my daytime prison.

At night, it became my hell.

Matthew woke at 3 a.m. He had cried throughout the previous evening and finally fell asleep near midnight. I nursed and changed him, but he still screamed, so I moved our disturbance downstairs to avoid waking Mike. Standing before the oak mantle in the living room, I looked in the mirror. It reflected a disheveled woman in a blue nightgown and a baby kicking his legs out of a drawstring sleeper. I turned away, humming *Silent Night* in the warm October gloom.

I imagined I looked calm as I caressed my red-faced infant, planting soft kisses on his nose and hands. Occasionally, I interrupted my hums with "Shhh." But inside, my control started to crack. How much crying could I take? How little sleep could I tolerate? How much pain could this baby endure, and how long could I endure witnessing it? My nipples stung, my back ached, my heart raced, my husband slept, my baby screamed.

A picture flashed through my mind. In it, I violently shook Matthew, his arms and legs and head whipping back and forth like a branch in a hurricane.

Silent night, holy night…

Holding Matthew up to the mirror, I asked him, "Who's that fussy baby?" He kicked harder, and another image invaded my thoughts—me, screaming in Matthew's face, "SHUT UP!"

All is calm, all is bright…

I picked up a rattle and jiggled it. Matthew hesitated a moment, then screamed even louder.

So tender and mild…

Upstairs, the toilet flushed, and footsteps crossed the hallway.

"Karen, is everything okay down there?" Mike called.

"We're fine. You go back to bed."

"You sure?"

"Yeah."

"Okay, love you, see you in the morning."

"Love you, too."

The bedroom door closed.

Every muscle in my body tensed while snapshots flashed in my mind. My hand covering Matthew's mouth. *Click.* Pressing too hard. *Click.* Muffling him for a moment, just a moment, long enough for some peace, just long enough for a breath of silence. *Click.*

I froze. I shuddered. Then I cried.

"Matthew, I love you," I whispered into his perfect ear, my mouth sticky with phlegm. "I'll never hurt you, I promise."

Shuffling into the kitchen to get a tissue, I again imagined my hand over Matthew's mouth—but not like the first time when the scene popped into my head. I revisited the moment intentionally, and disgust quivered up my spine. *Is this what it's like when parents hurt their children? Is this how it starts? We're not so different, they and I.* Humbled, I said a silent prayer for all the parents in the world.

Finally, Matthew cried himself out, as did I. I put him back in his crib, and leaned over, resting my hands and chin on the rail. *How could this beautiful baby, this flesh-of-my-flesh, conjure such a beast within me?*

Every day since Matthew's birth, I had worried about waking one morning to find him lifeless and blue in his crib, dead from SIDS or some other horrible malady. But now, any end seemed better than Matthew's constant agony and my inability to comfort him. Succumbing to these dark thoughts, I found myself bargaining with God:

Was this a mistake, God? If it wasn't meant to be, I'll accept it. I've had a chance to be a mom; I've nurtured and nourished this baby. But it's not working, and I understand if you have to take him. Then, next time, I'll do it right. Next time, I'll be prepared. I'll have the baby I was meant to have. I'll be the mom I was meant to be.

I thought I was alone. I didn't know other new mothers experienced intrusive thoughts like mine, or extreme sadness, anxiety, and exhaustion. I didn't know I could have been diagnosed and treated.

Although public awareness of postpartum depression (PPD) began to pick up steam in the second half of the 1980s, I had missed the wave. If Drs. Spock or Brazelton addressed the serious mood disorder in the baby books, I must have skipped over it-it would never happen to me. Had I read about it and paid attention, I could have later pointed to a page and told Mike, "Look. I think I have this." I could have talked to my doctor who would have prescribed rest and support and a break from the baby. The scribbled words from a higher authority would have done what I could not: advocate for myself.

But would I have shared my secret? Would I have admitted to fantasies of smothering Matthew or smashing him against the wall or throwing him out the window? As it was, I never told anyone. Since moving away from our college friends, I hadn't rebuilt a circle of confidantes. And I wasn't good about picking up the phone to stay in touch. The only person I might have disclosed my struggles to was my mother, but I was too ashamed to admit my gruesome thoughts even to her. To come clean would have exposed me as an unworthy parent, unlikeable at best and unlovable at worst. Plus, I feared Matthew being taken from me, losing my husband, my family, my job. Therefore, I rationalized. I would never really hurt my child, so no one needed to know.

Years later, I discovered Anne Lamott's 1993 memoir *Operating Instructions*. In it, she writes of her three-week-old,

"I have had some terrible visions lately, like of holding him by the ankle and whacking him against the wall." Lamott bumbled through her son's first year with grace and humor. Where was her voice when I had needed it?

After a four-month maternity leave, I returned to work in mid-December. On my first day back, Mike dropped Matthew off at daycare, and I arrived at the library before my coworkers. Pulling open the heavy wood doors, I stomped the snow off my boots and stepped inside. Soft lights warmed the lobby. Neat stacks of books and papers sat on my desk in the far corner, my chair pulled out as if waiting for me. I stood still for a moment, breathing in the scent of old books and dusting spray, inhaling the silence. I thought of all the mothers I'd read about who struggle with separation anxiety that first day back to work. Not me. I stood in a working mother's heaven. When my colleagues arrived, they welcomed me back and consoled me about having to leave the baby. Embarrassed to admit my truth, I simply nodded and agreed.

One morning early in February, I woke with a start, looked at the alarm clock, and gasped. It was 5 a.m. Matthew had slept through the night. *Or….*

I jumped out of bed and ran to his room. He breathed peacefully, but I kept my hand lightly on his chest until my trembling stopped.

At six months old, Matthew's colic finally abated, and he

started sleeping seven or more hours most nights. I had stopped breastfeeding at around four and a half months, disappointed I couldn't last longer. Working full-time and hand-expressing milk, however, proved to be more than I could handle. The extra sleep worked wonders, and I finally understood what the baby books described as "falling head over heels in love with your child."

One night, Mike and I checked on Matthew before we went to bed and found him lying on his side in his crib, one arm thrown protectively over his Teddy. I couldn't walk away from the perfect scene. It belonged on a magazine cover with the caption, "*This* is why people have babies."

I sang endlessly, inventing songs and taking artistic liberties. Matthew, not Michael, rowed his boat ashore. And how could anyone sing to their child about a baby and its cradle crashing down? No wonder kids had nightmares. Instead, I gave "Rock-a-bye Baby" new lyrics: "When the wind blows, the baby will smile, cuz Mommy loves Matthew, mile after mile."

Matthew hit all the remaining first year milestones on time—crawling, cruising, running (because walking apparently wasn't his thing), his blond curls bouncing with every step. Oh, those blond curls! Why did I ever cut them? I saved the clippings in a plastic baggie, and after that first trim, Matthew's hair grew straighter and darker like his father's.

One day when Matthew was sixteen months old, Mike and I sat in the car at a traffic light.

"T! T!" Matthew chirped from the back seat.

"Is he saying T like the letter T? Mike asked.

"But I don't see a T anywhere," I said, looking around.

Then I looked at the big truck next to us and there it was, a capital letter T prominently displayed in the company's name.

Matthew started finding Ts everywhere—on magazine covers, baby food jars, diaper boxes—wowing us with his precociousness. We christened him our "Little Einstein."

On Saturdays, Matthew woke at dawn. I would have traded a day's pay for an extra hour of sleep, but I got up so Mike could snooze. By the time Matthew was two, we had a routine. I dragged out the mixing bowl and stood Matthew on a little table next to the counter so he could stir the batter for oat bran muffins. After I popped the trays in the oven, I snapped a bib around his neck and gave him the mixing spoon to lick. When he got a little older, I taught him how to measure flour by lightly spooning it into a cup and leveling it off with the flat blade of a butter knife.

"Get ready," I whispered to Matthew when I heard Mike coming down the steps.

"Surprise, Daddy!" we yelled.

"Yook it, Daddy. Muppins!" Matthew exclaimed, his face bursting with pride.

Evenings after Matthew was in bed, Mike and I often sat on our tiny deck with a drink, the baby monitor close at hand.

"Did you see that shooting star?" Mike asked one night.

"No, I had my eyes closed." But in my mind, I had been gazing at the night sky, filled with peace and promise, basking in my blessings.

Long moments passed in silence.

"It's so still," I said.

"Yeah," Mike replied. "Isn't it great?"

It *was* great. I drained my glass of chardonnay, looked up at the moon cresting over the trees in the park next door and proclaimed, as I often did, "I love our life."

6

When He was Good...

Soon after Matthew turned two, I left my library job and accepted a health education position with the county Cooperative Extension office. My responsibilities included teaching nationally acclaimed parenting programs like *Discipline is not a Dirty Word*. As a result, I took credit for the daily happy faces on Matthew's daycare report and his hop-skip-jumping over the "terrible twos." I practically huffed on my fingernails and shined them on my lapel.

My bubble of self-righteousness popped when Matthew invented the "horrible fours." Well-behaved at daycare, Matthew let loose the minute he got home. He bounced from room to room, couch to chair, toy to toy, too full of energy to listen. We avoided taking him to public places where he'd surely be disruptive.

One Saturday, however, Matthew and I piled into my neighbor Janis's minivan with her two kids to see *The Little Mermaid* at the New York State Museum. A stay-at-home mom, Janis took her kids everywhere—kiddie concerts, Ice Capades, apple-picking, hot air balloon-watching. When she invited us to the movies, I felt ashamed to admit how little we took Matthew out, so I said yes.

The cavernous stone and marble lobby echoed with the chatter, giggles, and whining of scores of children. As we stood in line, Matthew kicked up his legs with glee like a baby goat in springtime. Gripping his hand, I quietly but firmly reminded him, "Feet on the floor, Matthew." When he laughed and whooped, I admonished him to "Use your inside voice." Then he grabbed the red velvet rope and swung it like a jump rope, its arc matching his smile. Heat rose in my face when I saw the other parents' sideways sneers. Matthew was *that* child in the crowd, and I was *that* mother who couldn't control him. "Matthew. MATTHEW," I repeated, taking his chin in my hand. When he finally looked at me, I glared back. "Look. With. Your. Eyes."

As soon as I let go, he gave a Rockettes-worthy kick, hitting the heavy base holding the velvet rope. It toppled, threatening to pull all the other ropes and bases down with it, and I caught it just before it crashed to the floor. If I had driven us in my car, I would have stalked out, dragging my rollicking son behind me. But I was at the mercy of Janis, who pretended not to notice the commotion. I took Matthew aside and squatted down to his level. "Stop it. Right now. Or we will never go to a movie again." And we didn't, not for several years, even though he sat through *The Little Mermaid* as quiet as a clam.

One night later in the week, Matthew set up his yellow racetrack on the living room carpet and dumped out his bin of vehicles. He lay on his stomach, knees bent, bare feet sticking up in the air. I tickled them and sat down to play.

I pushed a red VW Beetle around the track, pretending to have fun. "Vroom, vroom," I said, thinking how much I'd prefer playing with a Barbie Doll.

Matthew crashed two cars together and threw them into the air.

"Matthew, cars drive on the floor."

He ignored me, throwing more cars around the room, falling backward with sound effects.

"If that happens again, we will put the cars away."

But the chaos escalated. When a silver Corvette t-boned the ceiling, I announced time-out, and took Matthew firmly by the arm into the kitchen. The parenting books said if a child won't sit in time-out, it was okay to hold them there. They didn't say what to do when the child giggled and squirmed and flopped like a rag doll, making him impossible to hold.

"Do you need to go upstairs to your room, Matthew?"

"Nooooo," he howled, wagging his head back and forth.

"Then. Get. Into. The. Chair."

"Nooooo."

"I'm going to count to three…"

Before I reached "two," Matthew had wiggled out of my grasp. I grabbed him, carried him upstairs, plunked him down in his room, and quickly stepped out. His door had no lock, so I held the doorknob, which twisted and jiggled in my hand from the other side. Matthew screamed and cried, this time in anger. For a moment, he was quiet. Then—wild pounding against the door. *Was he kicking it?*

Afraid the solid wood door would splinter or get knocked

off its hinges, I opened it. Matthew lay on the floor on his back, sweaty and red-faced, both legs poised for another kick. He looked at me with surprise. I yanked off his shoes and shut the door behind me without saying a word. After a moment's pause, the kicking began again with a little less enthusiasm.

It seemed like hours but was probably all of ten minutes until Matthew finally calmed down. Fighting the urge to barge in and pummel him, I slid down against the door. What the hell was going on in my home?

None of my three younger brothers had been like this, not that I remember. None of the kids I babysat behaved this way. The only times I'd seen kids so out of control involved harried mothers in grocery stores or malls who swore and called their children names. Then, it was easy to mount my high horse and blame the child's misconduct on poor parenting. Now *I* was that mother at the end of her rope.

After a few minutes of quiet, I opened the door, sat cross legged on the floor and pulled Matthew into my lap, encircling him with a hug.

"Are you ready to talk about what happened?"

He nodded.

"You were really mad, weren't you Matthew?"

He nodded again.

"And what did you do with that madness?

"I threw cars."

"And what else?"

"I kicked the door."

"Yes. And what would have been a better thing to do when you're mad?"

"Use my words?"

"Yes. And I know next time you'll be much better at using your words, won't you?"

"Yes, Mommy."

"Do you have something to say to me?"

"I'm sorry."

"I love you, Matthew." I gave him a big squeeze.

"I love you too, Mommy." He squeezed me back.

After Mike got home, we inspected the deep gouges in the door, bewildered and perturbed at the rage and power they represented. When the scene repeated itself the following week, I barely had the physical strength to hold the door shut, so we installed a lock on the outside. It felt like I was caging my child.

When Matthew was a baby, Mike and I discussed our views on spanking. He didn't agree with it. I endorsed the philosophy I grew up with: physical punishment is warranted only when a child did something or was about to do something dangerous, like run into the street or touch a hot stove. In practice, I swatted Matthew on the behind much more often. Never hard enough to make him cry, but hard enough to slap me with a guilt trip. I believed spanking indicated my failure as a disciplinarian, my weakness as a mother. When I controlled my hand, but my brain ran wild with thoughts of smacking him across the face, I felt even guiltier.

Although Mike never spanked Matthew, he had as much difficulty disciplining him as me, his stern voice no match for our son's willfulness.

One particularly difficult night, I raised a troubling question.

"Mike, do you ever wonder what might have happened if Matthew had been born into another family? Like where the parents had no support system? Or they worked three jobs, or were super-stressed out?"

"You mean, what would happen to Matthew?"

"Yeah."

Mike pulled at his lips and looked away. "He may have been beaten."

I nodded in agreement, chilled to my core.

I thought about the parents who were court-ordered to attend my parenting classes, their faces red when I signed their attendance affidavit. I often saw myself standing in their shoes, sitting in their place, humiliation sinking me deep into the seat. Would a judge someday rule unfavorably against me? I wondered when and how and if that line would be crossed, if, someday, I would snap.

Mike and I talked about getting pregnant again. I refused to take that leap until we added a second bathroom, something we'd discussed as a good investment. I wanted to wash my hands on the first floor after a diaper change rather than running upstairs because Mike considered it gross to use the kitchen sink. And, although I'd always wanted two or three kids, I couldn't imagine caring for a baby in addition to Matthew, especially another baby *like* Matthew. I needed time. Mike began designing an addition, we took out a home equity loan, and, despite Matthew's challenging energy, I decided I wasn't "done." I wanted another chance at motherhood, another chance to do it right.

Just before Matthew turned five, on June 24, 1991, I got my second chance, my second son. When my parents, who had arrived earlier in the week, brought Matthew to the hospital, he held back for a moment. Then he gently, calmly crawled up next to me in bed where I cradled the baby. Matthew kissed me on the cheek. I pulled him into me and squeezed tightly.

"Matthew, this is Stephen." I placed the baby in his open arms. "You're a big brother now." Matthew stared for a moment, caressed Stephen's bald head, and kissed him on the forehead.

Twice, I have known what it's like to look at the brand-new face of the tiny creation I pushed into the world. Twice, I have seen the awe on my husband's face as he held the baby who shared his DNA. Twice, I have studied my mother's face, trying to imagine what it was like to see her daughter, who just yesterday, it must seem, popped into the world, now holding the child from her own womb.

The look on Matthew's face when he first held Stephen eclipsed those other moments, his expression a unique blend of innocence, wonder, awe, and pride. I had seen new siblings together in friends' photos and videos. I had seen them in movies. This was different. This was more than a smile, more than a demeanor. Matthew had an aura. Love overtook him. *My wild child was tame.*

At home a few days later, as I nursed Stephen in bed, Matthew came to the door and stood there, watching.

"C'mon in, Matthew." He padded over and leaned against the mattress, his face placid, eyes deep and serious. I could see he was working out something in his head. With a big sigh, he looked up.

"Mommy, I guess you won't need me anymore now that

you have Stephen, right?"

My heart collapsed.

"Oh honey." I freed an arm to tousle his hair. "We still need you! How could we ever be happy without you?" I placed Stephen in the bassinet, patted the bed for Matthew to climb up, and pulled him into my arms. "No one could ever replace you, Matthew. You were my first baby, and no other baby can ever take that away. Will you promise me you'll never forget how much I love you?"

"I promise."

As his body sank into mine, I vowed to double my efforts to show Matthew how much he was loved.

I pledged to love my sons equally—each with all my heart—but it was hard not to make comparisons. When Stephen fussed, I calmed him. When he cried, I knew how to stop the tears. At long last, I had the mother's touch. I told friends, "God gave me Stephen," but I didn't tell them how often I had felt utterly incompetent with Matthew, and that with Stephen, I felt redeemed.

The expense of infant daycare on top of afternoon care for Matthew's half-day kindergarten was unaffordable, so Mike and I agreed I should resign my health education job. I worried about being stuck at home all day caring for my newborn and his big brother, the Energizer Bunny, but a funny thing happened: Matthew's behavior improved. He still had energy enough to power a small city, but, like a generator, it was purposeful.

In our big fenced-in backyard, Matthew's long lean legs

carried him through the air in leaps and bounds from fencepost to fencepost. "Like a gazelle," I often told Mike. Wearing his Superman pajamas, Matthew was faster than a speeding tricycle, more powerful than a third grader, and able to leap tall rocks in a single bound. Some days, he preferred his Batman PJs. The Caped Crusader was agile and daring on our swing set and jungle gym, too much for my comfort, but I tried to let him determine his own limits. When I sat on the deck with Stephen, I held up his tiny finger and pointed it to Matthew. "Look at your big brother go!"

A video Mike took around this time shows Stephen lying on a blanket on the living room carpet. Matthew dances in circles around his brother, leaping, bouncing, twisting, and turning with joyful abandon. During every revolution, Matthew plops down to plant a kiss on Stephen's forehead, rub his tummy, or wiggle his tiny toes. "Hi, Stephen," Matthew whispers in a singsong voice as his brother stares back intently. Then he flies off, his skinny arms and legs flailing in all directions. "Matthew, MATTHEW," I repeat to get his attention, "Sit here for a minute, honey." Matthew bounces over and snuggles up to me for a kiss. But his joy isn't contained for long. Within moments, he springs up again, flitting from his little brother to a pile of blocks to the empty baby carrier to the playpen to me. In the final seconds of the video, Mike pans the camera to my face. I look exhausted.

Shortly after Matthew started first grade in 1992, when Stephen was one, I returned to work, accepting a position as an elementary school Student Assistance Counselor. In that role funded by the Rensselaer County Department of Mental Health, I worked in an elementary school, primarily teaching a healthy living curriculum in K-5 classrooms. I also ran student support groups and occasionally met one-on-one with children to assess their need for additional mental health services. Despite the title, the position was less counselor than educator, which suited my background and skills. The twelve-month position included an attractive perk--I could flex my hours and use accrued comp time on school holidays and summers. This became the start of what I later called our Golden Years, when life was a reasonable balance of work I loved and family I loved more.

Every August, I attended two weeks of mandatory training with my team of elementary and upper grade counselors, culminating with a family picnic. One year, I promised to bring apple crisp, and I told the boys they could help.

I cleared the ugly laminate counter in the kitchen, picking up a handful of McDonald's Happy Meal toys, a loose wheel from a plastic truck, and a broken pencil imprinted with "Matthew."

"Matthew, Stephen!" I called. "Time for apple crisp!"

With a clatter of Mr. Potato Head parts from the living room, they came running. Matthew bounded into the room first, and I smoothed his hair and kissed him on his forehead.

"Go wash your hands in the bathroom."

"Okay, Mom." He danced out of the room singing, "Apple crisp, apple crisp."

Stephen ran into the room mimicking his older brother. "Apple cips, apple cips." I grabbed him and tickled his belly. He squealed.

"You love helping Mommy, don't you?" He hugged me in response.

I pulled the brown kiddie table over to the sink and helped Stephen climb up to wash his hands. Then I clamped the apple-corer/peeler to the counter and began cranking out the long, continuous peels my boys gobbled up. Most of the nutrients in an apple lay just under the skin, and I was happy to indulge their tastes.

While the apple crisp baked in the oven, I cleaned up. The boys returned to their pile of potato body parts, and I joined them on the floor just as Mike walked in the door.

"It smells great in here!"

The boys ran to greet him, and I got up to kiss him as well. For a few minutes we group-hugged. The harder Matthew and Stephen squeezed, the more they laughed, instigating Mike and I to join in. Wrapped in love, my heart swelled.

7

Dividing Lines

In February 1994, Mike suddenly and without effort lost twenty pounds. *Doesn't it figure,* I thought. *Without him even trying.* We blamed it on his endless weekend house projects when he rarely stopped for lunch.

A few days later, Mike called me into the bathroom. "I lost five more."

My eyes followed his finger pointing to the scale, and it took a moment for the number to register over the whirr of the bathroom fan and the dissipating scent of Irish Spring. I looked up slowly. Mike has a slight build, which made his weight loss noticeable. Naked but for his plaid boxers, he looked drawn. His ribs showed.

I made him promise to call his doctor first thing Monday morning, and for the rest of the day, we didn't mention it or discuss our fears. Cancer was mine. What else could it be?

"Diabetes, type 1."

Mike slumped inside the front door after three days of tests. His glasses fogged, and chunks of dirty snow melted from his boots. "That's the bad kind."

I pulled him into an embrace, shocked but secretly relieved. *Diabetes? We can do diabetes.*

That night, the boys asleep, Mike and I sat on his side of our bed surrounded by pamphlets, packages, and white pharmacy bags. He looked defeated, hunched over like an old man.

"Type 1 is insulin-dependent diabetes. It's what they used to call juvenile onset diabetes," he explained. "Without insulin, you die."

His words loomed over me like an oppressive cloud, and I sank into the mattress from the pressure. Mike said it was rare for adults, especially those without a family history, to be diagnosed with type 1diabetes.

"That's why it took them a few days to figure out what was wrong." He turned to me, eyes pleading. "I'm thirty-six, for God's sake."

Within a day, Mike shed his despondency. He appeared to thrive on the self-care and his new toys—a blood meter, syringes, vials of insulin. He showed Matthew, seven, and Stephen, two, how his blood glucose meter worked and let Matthew push the buttons. Both kids watched their father give himself injections and "milk" his finger for a drop of blood.

"Daddy is taking very good care of himself," he told the boys. "I won't let my disease make me sick." Mike vowed to manage his diabetes so well, it would not shorten his life even a day. I vowed to support him.

Despite Mike's discipline, however, we faced a steep learning curve. One day, shortly after his diagnosis, Mike helped me unpack grocery bags in the kitchen after I came home from shopping.

"Karen, something weird happened while you were out. I saw stars."

I stopped, frozen orange juice concentrate halfway to the freezer, and stared at him. At that moment, his face had good color, his hands steady. Only the downturned corners of his mouth gave away his fear.

"I was wrestling on the floor with Stephen, and all of a sudden, I saw bright flashes." Mike balled his hands and opened them quickly to illustrate. "It was just like in cartoons. They were floating around in my peripheral vision."

"Whoa," I said quietly, shutting the freezer door. It didn't sound like a huge deal to me, but Mike was clearly freaked out, and he knew more about diabetes than I did.

He believed it was a low blood sugar reaction, a new symptom for us to remember, along with tingling lips, shakiness, and a yellow pallor to his face, which I usually noticed before he was aware his sugar had dropped.

What if he had gone into insulin shock and passed out? What if something had happened to Stephen? I had seen *Steel Magnolias*. I knew the worst-case scenario.

Taking a bag of apples from his hands, I hugged him and asked, "What did Stephen do?"

"He didn't know. I made sure of that. I just told him Daddy was tired."

It took over a year for Mike to feel comfortable getting on the floor to play with the boys again. He held back, cautious not to overexert himself. I decided that for a while, major parenting responsibilities would be mine. As always, I'd do anything to make Mike happy. Now, I'd do anything to keep him alive.

Mike's diagnosis was a dividing line, a concept people often use when talking about a serious illness, accident, or life-changing event. Before the divorce. Before the cancer. After he died. Most people have many such notable events, not all of them tragic. Before and after births, weddings, coming-out, moving, fame, or fortune. Even the addition of a family pet is significant when seen through the lens of change.

In the spring, I had the bright idea that a four-legged family member would be good for the boys, and I believed we could manage the added responsibility. Mike agreed. On a rainy Saturday, we pulled up to the outdoor pet adoption day at the animal shelter.

Wet-dog smell permeated the car when Mike got out to investigate. Matthew unlocked his seatbelt, and I unbuckled Stephen from his car seat. We peered through the windows.

"Stephen, see all the dogs?"

He pointed out the window. "Goggies!"

Matthew leaned toward Stephen. "Maybe Daddy will find us a doggie to bring home. It will be our very own pet." He took Stephen's hands and clapped them together. "Say 'yay,' Stephen."

"Yay!" they yelled in unison.

In a soggy field, Mike grabbed the leash of a large golden and white Labrador retriever mix. As he struggled to control her, the dog leapt at people, jerked away from the leash, and pulled in every direction. *Don't even think about it,* I mentally telegraphed.

Mike handed the dog back and strutted to the car. I rolled down my window a few inches.

"Karen, did you see that beautiful dog I was walking?"

"Yeah, it looks too aggressive. You had a hard time controlling it."

"It really wasn't bad. I put my hand right in front of her face and she didn't nip or anything. She's beautiful, isn't she?"

"Yes. She is pretty." *He can't be serious. What is he thinking?*

Matthew and Stephen wrestled in the back seat, jabbering about dogs.

"Do you want to walk her, Karen? To see what you think?"

I didn't want to, but I said, "Sure."

Mike never forced me to do anything. It wasn't his nature. He never gave me or withheld his permission, and I never asked his permission or felt I needed to. But Mike had a way of stating an opinion as if it were a universal truth, and I had a way of going along. "A salad isn't a salad without tomatoes," he said. "It's just wrong." So even if we had lettuce, cucumbers, croutons, and olives, if we had no tomatoes, we had no salad. "Store brand mayo is a crime. It's Hellman's or nothing." So I bought Hellman's, although it cost fifty cents more.

When we took the boys out for ice cream and Mike perused the menu, he often announced to no one in particular, "You can't eat soft-serve. Real ice cream is scooped from the freezer."

I loved the creamy texture of soft serve ice-cream. I loved it in a bowl, every sweet mouthful eaten with a spoon so I could savor the experience without worrying about a mess dripping down my arm. I should have told Mike *You don't know what you're missing,* as I ordered an extra-large chocolate-vanilla swirl and ate it slowly in front of him to make my point. Instead, I stopped eating soft serve, even if Mike were nowhere around.

At the pet adoption, Mike couldn't step outside of himself to see what a disaster this dog would be. Caught up in childlike excitement, he lost sight of reality. I should have been adult enough to say *no*. But I was used to going along with Mike and not thinking for myself.

With the powerfully wild dog on the leash, I exerted all my will and physical strength to try to maintain control. When I returned to the car and expressed doubt to Mike, he delivered the key sales pitch: "It's your choice, Karen." That was the clincher. He didn't need to pontificate about why this was the best or only dog for our family. I knew what he wanted, and I knew if I said no, *I* would be the bad guy. If we drove home empty-handed, it would be *my* fault. Mike wouldn't make me feel that way; he didn't need to. I paved my own guilt trip.

Does blame lie at the feet of the person who doesn't see the problem, or the person who sees the problem and doesn't speak up?

The boys named her Lissy, short for Felicity, her given name. At home, Mike put his hand in her food bowl to test her aggression, exclaiming what a good dog she was not to nip or snarl. He helped Stephen feed her out of his hand, again exclaiming how good she was. Mike told anyone who would listen about our good dog, Lissy. Yet she was so unruly on her leash, even Mike had trouble controlling her.

Before we had signed the papers, the adoption organizers suggested we take Lissy to dog obedience. I figured if I couldn't handle her, the adoption wasn't going to work, so I took on the challenge. Twice a week for a month, I tried to get that dog to behave. The instructor recommended we buy a training collar that looked like a medieval torture device, yet even that didn't tame Lissy. I developed a mean alpha-male voice as advised, and I warned the kids before I used it so it wouldn't scare them. Channeling all my frustration and anger into two words, I screamed, "LISSY NO!" It got the dog's attention but made my heart pound and my throat ache.

One Saturday when Mike was running errands, my neighbor Janis's kids came over to play outside. I watched from the deck, sipping iced tea. When my kids were in the yard, I couldn't *not* watch. What if they got hurt? What if they needed me, and I wasn't immediately there? Even indoors, until Matthew and Stephen were three or four and could play independently, I rarely let them out of my sight. I never discovered them scribbling on the walls or unrolling the toilet paper because I was always watching. I worried they'd pull the child-proof outlet covers off and poke a toy in. Or, despite our ban on toys small enough to swallow, they'd find a button and choke. Outdoors, the risks were magnified. What if a stranger climbed the fence and took off with my children?

Lissy ran in large circles around the kids where they romped in the yard. Then her circles grew smaller and smaller. I stood up with concern.

Suddenly, the dog charged at little Nicole, grabbing her skinny thigh in her mouth as if it were a stick.

"LISSY, NO!" I jumped off the deck. Lissy let go and took off.

"Get up on the swing set!" I yelled. The kids scrambled to comply.

When I caught Lissy, I snapped on her leash and exploded

at her. "BAD DOG, LISSY, BAD DOG!" I shook, near tears. Nicole barely had a scratch, but it horrified me to think what might have happened. Furious with Mike for not seeing past his "good dog" blinders, I was even angrier at myself for not standing up to him.

As soon as Mike came home, I told him what had happened. In a rare moment of self-assuredness, I looked him in the eye.

"This. Dog. Has. To. Go."

"But she's such a good—"

"If you love this dog so much, you're going to have choose between her and me."

He half-smiled, half-chuckled, playing with the keys in his hand. He thought I was joking.

"Me or the dog," I repeated, staring him down. I pictured myself moving out of the house to make my point.

Mike called the shelter on Monday. End of problem, end of story...for him. But my shame lingered—that my instinct had screamed, *Danger! Danger!* yet I said nothing. That danger became near disaster before I let my voice be heard. That I couldn't speak up even when a child's health and wellness were at stake.

Matthew's eye-rolling tic became the final dividing line of 1994, what I later came to call "the beginning of the end of the old Matthew." Since Mike was still adjusting to his new diagnosis, I kept most of my concerns about Matthew to myself. I allowed Mike to push the tic oddity to the recesses of his subconscious, to let it be a pea that rolled under the stove, there but forgotten. For me, the eye-rolling was a daily, in-my-face reminder, like the penny Mike helped Matthew press into the fresh concrete steps in front of our house. I couldn't *not* see it.

After Dr. Peterson told me not to worry about Matthew's "habit tic," she asked about any new concerns in the family.

"As a matter of fact, we did have a surprise over the winter," I said. "My husband was diagnosed with type 1 diabetes." Dr. Peterson raised her eyebrows, so I assured her. "He's really doing well, though. He's *so* disciplined."

"That was a shock, I'm sure." Dr. Peterson picked up her clipboard and pen. "Matthew's probably anxious about his father. Don't you think?"

No, I didn't. But she didn't let me answer.

"I think some family counseling would be beneficial."

I *knew* Matthew wasn't anxious about Mike's diagnosis. Even in the middle of a low blood sugar reaction, Mike was stoic. The kids never suspected a thing. I knew my child, and I knew he didn't fret about his father. But as a counselor, I didn't want to appear distrustful of my own occupation.

"I'll talk to my husband."

When I suggested the idea to Mike and Matthew, they both balked, so I dropped it.

The therapeutic relationship wasn't new to me. As early as sixteen, I saw a counselor for my low self-esteem and what may have been undiagnosed depression. In college and afterward, I periodically sought out the support of mental health specialists. I valued personal growth and relished the purposeful attention on me. The one topic I skirted was my relationship with food.

In my undergraduate psychology courses, I inhaled every chapter, article, and research study on eating disorders. But anorexia was not even remotely my experience and bulimia didn't fit because I didn't intentionally purge. The literature didn't describe the way I sometimes binged on cookies, candy bars, or sweet cereal until I felt sick. It didn't name the power a leftover crust of pie had over me.

As early as 1959, the medical literature recognized binge eating, described as "an eating pattern marked by consuming large amounts of food at irregular intervals." But "binge eating disorder" was not included as its own disorder in the American Psychiatric Association's *Diagnostic and Statistical Manual of Mental Disorders*, the *DSM*, until 2013. "Pigging out" was the best description I had for what I did.

When I finally opened up to a therapist about my eating, I knew he'd be disgusted by my habits. I couldn't imagine telling him, for example, about my after-work detours when I stopped at three different gas stations or convenience stores for binge food. I didn't purchase enough at any one stop to arouse suspicion, just a jumbo peanut butter cookie, perhaps, and a bag of peanut M&Ms—or two bags, one for a "friend." Like a thin person might buy. Then I ate quickly as I drove to the next stop where I threw away the wrappers before feeding my habit again. My third and final stop usually included a cup of coffee to combat the inevitable carbohydrate coma.

I bought the cheapest, junkiest of junk foods. Since binges at times lasted for days or continued on and off for weeks or months, pricier brands were cost prohibitive. Taste was irrelevant anyway when I shoveled food in as quickly as I did.

At times I knew what triggered a binge. The phone call from a student's mother, irate that I had called child protective services. Mike's traveling for work. An over-scheduled family calendar, or, conversely, momentary boredom. More often, though, the impetus escaped me. I couldn't see it then, but the binge-instigator was usually an accumulation of unexpressed emotions and unmet needs buried in my subconscious. Without realizing it, I self-medicated with food in failed attempts to keep the disagreeable parts of life at bay.

8

Matthew's Terrible, Horrible, Zero

Matthew entered third grade shortly after his eye-rolling began. About a month into the school year, I sent in a note asking his teacher to call us to set up a meeting.

"Before we talk," I asked Mrs. Murphy when she called, "do you notice anything unusual about Matthew?"

She answered without hesitation. "The involuntary tic."

There it was—confirmed. Matthew's eye-rolling was obvious. But I really wanted to discuss homework, so we set a date to meet.

The guiding principle for elementary school homework was ten minutes per night per grade. Since his kindergarten half-days, when coloring and tracing should have taken five minutes or less, our smart, silly, fidgety son made a mockery of the guidelines.

One evening, when Matthew was in second grade, I left

him at the kitchen table working on a math sheet while I put Stephen to bed. When I came back, Matthew sat on the blue loveseat, absorbed in a book, and I couldn't stop myself from reacting. "Matthew, there's no time to read! You have homework to do!" The moment the words left my mouth, I wanted to climb into the motherhood doghouse. Yet, what could I do? I didn't want *Alexander's Terrible, Horrible, No Good, Very Bad Day* to become *Matthew's Big Fat Bright Red Zero.*

Matthew's third grade homework, including assignments for the gifted program he joined that year, should have taken him forty-five minutes, but we spent almost two hours on it every night. The material wasn't difficult for Matthew. Even with Mike or me sitting with him, though, his attention wandered, and confusion reigned.

When the demands on our time and Matthew's ability to focus were simply too much, Mike and I tried to convince him to leave some work uncompleted. "We'll write you an excuse," we promised. But Matthew wouldn't hear of it. He may have feared his teacher's disapproval, but he also had an internal drive to do his best, the same compulsion that kept him in the good graces of his daycare teachers when he was four.

The following week, Mike and I folded ourselves into undersized chairs in Mrs. Murphy's classroom. Popsicle stick houses in varying states of collapse lined up across the radiator, which let out an occasional hiss. As I watched, wet splotches on the freshly washed blackboards dried to a chalky film. Waddling over to her desk, Mrs. Murphy leaned against it, resting her hand on her very pregnant belly. She picked up a handful of papers and fanned her red face, laughing loudly. "Don't mind me. Just havin' a hot flash. But don't worry, I'll only be out for eight weeks."

Mrs. Murphy recommended we use a timer at home, as she would in school, to keep Matthew on task. "My background is special ed," she said. "I'm very comfortable with students who learn differently. And I'll make sure my maternity sub follows our plan."

Poof. My worries disappeared. Not only did Matthew's teacher have the training to help him and the willingness to expend the extra effort, but I didn't need to assert myself to ask for special treatment.

The next day, I bought two timers—one for us and one for Mrs. Murphy. It was a way to say we appreciated her support, that we were responsible and generous parents. Mostly, it was my way of saying, "Like me," because if she liked me, she would take good care of Matthew.

I knew our home environment needed to be more conducive to Matthew's concentration. Mike didn't see how our perpetual whole-house DIY mess made any difference, but I knew it mattered. I felt it myself.

When Matthew was in first grade, we renovated the larger bedroom to be shared by the boys. Matthew had picked yellow paint, outer space wallpaper, and an astronaut border. "He needs a desk," I told Mike when homework became a bigger drag in third grade. So Mike built a desk to fit in the alcove created by a dormer window, and Matthew helped him paint it deep-space blue. It was perfect. The answer to our problem, I was sure.

As the year wore on, Matthew's biological engine slowly, inexplicably downshifted. He became less squirmy, more serene; less hyper, more daydreamy. I barely got used to the change, thoroughly enjoying the new calm, when, like the U.S.S. Enterprise, Matthew shifted into hyperdrive. Then, after an hour or two, he returned to his baseline again, which dipped lower and lower as the months passed. He was still easily distracted, but keeping him on task took less containment, more stimulation.

"Needs improvement" now littered Matthew's report cards. His straight A's since kindergarten became majority B's, although he continued to make honor roll each quarter. Mike and I placed little value on third grade academic awards, but grades and honor roll provided metrics to assess Matthew's progress or lack thereof. Despite his drop in achievement indicators, Mrs. Murphy wrote on his final report card, "I am very pleased with his academic performance."

Matthew's repertoire of near-continuous tics grew to include pursed lips, knitted eyebrows, and a wrinkled nose. When they all happened together, Mike and I called it "face-scrunching" between ourselves and turned our backs to fight back laughter. I fought back guilt, too, for laughing at my child.

I also wrestled with fear. Before we had children, Mike and I talked about kids getting teased.

"It happens to everyone," he said. "It's part of growing up."

"I never want our kids to be teased by anyone," I said, horrified at the thought.

I believed a mother should protect her children from pain, that I indeed *would* protect my future children. Flashing back to the shame I felt as a teen when I got teased for being fat, I cringed to think the same thing might happen to my own off-spring. I never wanted them to suffer. I hadn't figured out yet that pain is part of life, that challenges present opportunities, that we can choose not to internalize others' opinions.

For most of my years at Nativity Catholic elementary school in Pittsburgh, I didn't think much about popularity. I was chubbier than most of the girls in my class, but didn't care. By seventh grade, I understood that I wasn't one of the "in" girls, and I wished I were, but it didn't affect my self-esteem. After eighth grade, the school's protective shell cracked as graduates scattered. I attended the large public high school where girls were prettier, thinner, and sexier than me, and they and the boys knew it. I felt I had nothing to offer the cool-girl cliques and couldn't imagine any boy looking twice at me. My self-confidence crashed and my weight mushroomed. I dieted, lost weight, and gained it all back again. Each upswing of the scale plunged my self-esteem deeper into a hole.

I didn't want this for my children. It pained me to think Matthew's tics might damage his ego as my weight had damaged mine. And deeper down, beneath layers of self-loathing, lay an old, crusty ache for myself. Matthew's tics made him different. They made him odd—which made me the mother of the odd kid. Once again, I wouldn't be cool, this time by association with my child.

I often consulted my counselor colleagues about Matthew. Although each of us worked in separate schools and school districts, our teams met regularly and bonded tightly, filling my friendship void. Over time, I'd come to tell this group of compassionate, knowledgeable professionals private thoughts, fears and dreams I wouldn't tell my own family. We all had master's degrees, and most of the high school contingent were licensed clinical social workers, experts in child behavioral health. The team's consensus on Matthew's tics: "nothing to worry about." One colleague even pulled out a reference book and showed me in black and white that habit tics commonly appear around age eight and usually disappear within a year or two. As if to prove the theory, I noticed more and more children at my own school displaying an assortment of tics. I concluded my colleagues were right.

Then I attended a work seminar in August 1995. In a stuffy conference room, over the hum of an ineffective air conditioner, I chatted with my teammates as we waited for the presentation to begin. I expressed my biggest concern for the upcoming school year—that Matthew's tics would make him the butt of fourth-grade jokes.

The stocky man in a polo shirt standing at the front of the room wrote "ADHD—attention deficit hyperactivity disorder" on the chalkboard, and I settled a notebook on my lap.

As he addressed the causes, symptoms, and treatments of ADHD—a neurobehavioral disorder characterized by excess energy, compulsive behaviors, and distractibility—I mentally weighed each topic's relevance to what I observed at home. When Matthew was younger, I often wondered if he were clinically hyperactive. But, as an undergraduate, I had learned of a simple assessment: if a child can watch TV without interruption for thirty minutes, he was not hyperactive. With that in mind, I'd occasionally peek in on Matthew to find him sitting cross-legged on the carpet, his neck craned up, images from *Sesame Street* or *Reading Rainbow* casting flashes of light across his face. He barely moved. He could be anesthetized there for hours if we allowed it. I concluded that although Matthew was "hyper," he wasn't "hyperactive." When I ran my thoughts by Dr. Peterson, she had agreed.

The chalkboard bullet points about ADHD made me rethink my previous assumption. The next words made me rethink everything.

"ADHD is highly associated with a number of other disorders, one in particular that I find interesting." The presenter turned to the board and wrote "Tourette Syndrome."

I sat upright, riveted. An old episode of *L.A. Law* flashed through my mind. In it, a lawyer defended a client with Tourette Syndrome (also called Tourette's), a neurological disease that causes uncontrollable facial, motor, and vocal tics. The client, an intelligent man in a jacket and tie, bobbed his head, blinked his eyes, twitched his shoulders. Worse, he had coprolalia, an uncommon symptom that caused him to shout and swear inappropriately. "Bitch!" the defendant yelled from the witness stand when the female judge asked a question.

The clicking of pens and rustling of papers in the conference room faded away as I focused on the speaker's raspy voice and the harsh words scratched on the board. My brain put the pieces together. *Omigod, could Matthew have Tourette's?*

That evening, I told Mike about the seminar.

"Do you remember that *L.A. Law* show?" I asked.

"Yeah. But Matthew's tics are nothing like that. I don't even notice them that often."

I wanted to roll my eyes and ask him how the hell he could

miss the tics. Then I thought, *How could he* not *miss them?* He worked long hours to support our family. His business traveling and weekend commitments took him away from home. Every single day, he fought to manage a devastating disease. My complaints and Matthew's behaviors were like flies swarming Mike's head. He didn't exactly swat them away, but he closed his eyes in self-protection. I gave him a pass and held my tongue.

Since the day Matthew lay in his crib for the first time and his twitches, wheezes, and whimpers made me a worrier, I had tried to ignore my hypersensitive mind. Aware my thoughts quickly jumped to worst-case scenarios, I got in the habit of dimming my inner distress beacon. When its painfully bright light warned of Tourette's and ADHD, I blinked, signaling timidly for help, then turned down the light and looked away. I didn't call Dr. Peterson with my concerns. I was probably overreacting.

A month after Matthew started fourth grade, a stray dog found his way to our home and into our hearts, mine included this time. The boys, nine and four, named him Sparky, a fit moniker for the border collie mutt who barked relentlessly and raced around the yard herding snowflakes and butterflies. Fortunately, Sparky lacked Lissy's aggression, but Mike thought dog obedience might temper our pet's energy and teach Matthew responsibility. We signed him up with 4-H.

Matthew enjoyed training Sparky, and, although we didn't bond with the other families who had known each other for years, we were included in all of the group activities. For example, a class to make gingerbread houses, held in the home of a 4-H family in December.

The tantalizing scent of cinnamon and cloves greeted Matthew and me in the large, bright kitchen. Gingerbread pieces, bowls of white frosting, and assorted candy covered the counters, spilling onto card tables in the adjoining den. Hip grinding was Matthew's new tic, a provocative Michael Jackson-style move. I worried some little girl's mom would pull her daughter away, suspicious of this new boy's intentions. Admittedly, I would pull my daughter away, too, if I were her.

I tried to distract Matthew from his hip thrusts. "Here, hold this side until the frosting dries." Discreetly, I hooked my thumb in his pocket and pulled him toward me. "Don't do that," I whispered.

At home, I tried to understand what was going on.

"Matthew, do you have something scratchy in your underwear?"

"No."

"Is your penis hurting you?"

"No," he squealed, giggling. He tried to run away, but I caught him by the arm and tickled him. I laughed, too.

"Then why are you wiggling your butt around so much?"

He didn't know or couldn't say. Or maybe he wasn't aware he was doing it.

Finally, I told him not to wiggle when other people were around, that it was a private behavior only for home, and, gradually, Michael Jackson left the stage.

As fourth grade wore on, other odd behaviors appeared. Spitting, for example. Mike wasn't a spitter, thank goodness, so Matthew didn't learn the habit from him, but other boys and men practiced the behavior, and professional baseball players made a show of it. Disgusting as it was, I figured spitting was a rite of passage for males. Choosing my battles, I let it go.

Then one night, I came into Matthew's room to check on his homework. Bending down to kiss his head, I noticed tiny pools of water on the floor around his desk.

"Matthew, have you been spitting inside?"

"Yeah." I had to give him credit for being honest.

"That's not okay. If you really feel you have to spit, go into the bathroom or get a cup."

The next day, I noticed spit on his sweatshirt.

"Matthew, is that spit on your shirt?"

"Yeah. I had to spit, and I didn't want to spit on the floor and I didn't have a cup, so I spit on my shirt."

Growing up, I didn't often get in trouble or need to be reprimanded. The rules mostly felt fair, so I saw no reason to break them. Anyway, my mom's disappointment induced too much guilt and my dad's anger too much discomfort for me to risk misbehaving. When I disciplined my own kids, I never wanted them to feel bad for making a mistake. I tried not to come down too hard on them. But purposeful spitting on oneself crossed the line. It was too weird.

"No more spitting anywhere, Matthew. If you can't control it, then you can't do it at all." And it stopped. Never another spitting incident—inside, outside, in a cup, or on himself. That meant he had control over his behavior. Didn't he?

Then came the "wall art," pictures of spaceships etched with a pencil into the wall in his bedroom, accented with holes from thumbtacks. This from a child who never drew on the walls as a toddler. Immediately, I put a stop to it. Then another kind of art appeared all over the house—green, tacky things stuck to the walls. At first, I couldn't figure out what they were or where they came from. Then I realized, horrified, and stomped into Matthew's room.

"Matthew, have you been wiping boogers on the walls?"

"Yeah."

"Don't do that! Use a Kleenex!"

And it stopped.

Other behaviors seemed beyond Matthew's ability to control. If he got overly hungry, he became so silly and fidgety, we had trouble getting him to sit in a chair at the table. Once seated, he couldn't focus enough to get food into his mouth. So, with one hand firmly on Matthew's shoulder, Mike and I took turns feeding our nine-year-old like a baby until he settled down enough to take over.

Then he began resting his fingers in the food on his plate. Mike or I held Matthew's left hand down on the chair while he ate with his right hand, but as soon as we got distracted, the appendage wandered back to the trough. Finally, I taped a quarter underneath the glass kitchen table, a reward if Matthew kept his hand clean. He never made a cent.

I treated Matthew's behaviors like a person might react to a clump of new freckles on the back of her leg. *It's probably nothing*, she thinks. But she watches it. The clump gets a little bigger, so she looks up melanoma, feeling relieved it doesn't meet the criteria. Yet she keeps watching. When the clump gets darker, she twists her leg around and asks a loved one's opinion. "It's nothing," he says, but she reads up on skin cancer to be sure. When the clump gets bumpy, she sees a dermatologist who says, "It's nothing," and she tries to believe him. But she never stops watching.

When I talked about Matthew with friends or colleagues, I wondered if I painted an accurate portrait of my fourth grader. His peculiarities weren't all of him; they were only the dramatic highlights (or lowlights) in an otherwise ordinary life. Yet, they consumed me.

One day, I riffled through photo albums and boxes for a glimpse of the troubled son I depicted. He wasn't there. But I found a good-looking kid making silly faces with his little brother, two fingers held up surreptitiously behind Stephen's head. Matthew in a yellow slicker at Niagara Falls. Matthew sticking out his backside to the camera, a birthday-present-bow stuck to his butt. A werewolf who eerily resembled Matthew, with furry hands and chest hair, a heavy unibrow and black nose, snarling and slashing his claws at the camera.

Next, I scanned through our old video tapes. My problem child wasn't there, either. The boy immortalized on tape raked leaves into a pile and slid into it. He rode his bike, ran after Sparky, kicked the soccer ball, chased the hockey puck, spun on a disc down a snowy slope.

I felt confused but relieved. Matthew's days overflowed with happiness and fun, and the validation brought me tears of joy. Maybe I *was* being overly dramatic. Maybe Mike's inability to see the problem was twenty-twenty vision. Maybe when I brought Matthew to Dr. Peterson, she observed a personable, cooperative patient with a few habit tics accompanied by his anxious, overprotective mother. I swore that day to focus more on the good times.

Sniffling and satisfied, I put away the photos and all but one video tape that reminded me who the "real" Matthew was, renewing my hope for who he'd become.

The clip captured Matthew's magic act at the year-end school talent show. I remembered the preparation. Mike had helped him make shiny gold and red boxes with secret compartments, and I had sewn him a black cape with silver stars and moons. My parents were in town, and we all took our seats in the school cafetorium (a cafeteria with a stage at one end) where parents chatted, chairs scraped the floor, and the smell of day-old spaghetti lingered. After all the gymnastics routines, dance performances, and lip-synced Mariah Carey acts, the emcee introduced Matthew. The lights dimmed and a hush came over the room. In his black magician's attire, hair neatly slicked-back, Matthew gleamed like a silver coin pulled from behind an ear. With a wave of his wand, the magic began.

"For my first trick, I'll need a volunteer."

He announced this as if he did it every day. Then he strode down the stage steps and ambled through the audience. Sitting next to me, my dad (a pre-designated plant) raised his hand. Matthew tapped him on the shoulder, and they made their way to the stage, my dad's bushy gray hair bobbing up the aisle after his sorcerous grandson. The audience cheered them on.

"I need a crisp one-dollar bill," Matthew declared from his spot on stage. His "volunteer" conveniently pulled a dollar from his wallet and handed it over. The dollar disappeared in a gold box and reappeared in a red box, to the exaggerated gasps of my dad and the cheers of the audience. Dad returned to his seat and Matthew proceeded to his other sleight-of-hand tricks. Not all of them went smoothly, but Matthew was so self-possessed, funny, and charming, the audience loved him anyway. After his final bow, friends and acquaintances called over to me to compliment his performance. I soaked it all in, like sitting in a hot tub.

This confident, magical child was who I wanted the world to see. I knew he still existed, hidden behind the tics and odd behaviors, obscured by the homework struggles. I wanted to capture the moment in a bottle, to uncork when despair threatened to suffocate me, to sip when my mothering instincts became parched. The memories in the bottle would fill me from within, returning me to the hush of the room and the magic wand and my gleaming silver coin shining on the stage.

9

A Losing Prospect

A week before school started that fall, Mike insisted Matthew carry his bike down to the basement to put it away.

"Are you sure that's a good idea?" I asked, my eyes wide. Our veritable Superman, who had leapt tall rocks in his earlier years, now tripped and stumbled over his own two feet, increasingly prone to accidents.

"He's ten now, Mike said. "He's gotta learn to take responsibility."

I had read somewhere that mothers need to let fathers parent their sons as they see fit, as long as they're not abusive. I let Mike, an avid cyclist, impart his manly wisdom and exert his fatherly influence over our kids' bike riding. "Fresh air, exercise, always on my bike when I was a kid, blah, blah, blah." I kept my mouth shut, grateful our boys had a healthy role model to teach them how to conquer their fears and challenges, to teach them how to be tough. I didn't want my sons growing up soft like me.

When Matthew turned six or seven, I had started encouraging him to interact more independently with adults, to pay a cashier for his purchase or give a waitress his order. Matthew seldom resisted, but Stephen, when his time came, wanted no part of it, so I gave in and did things for him. After all, I reasoned, it's not like Stephen would be fifteen, still hiding behind my skirt while I bought his gummy bears or ordered his Big Mac. He'd learn eventually. What I didn't see until years later was that I had missed the whole point. The lesson wasn't about paying or ordering; it was about learning to face fear, to believe in yourself, to build new skills.

Mike stood on the gangway near the open side door. The inside landing led down nine steps to the basement and up three steps to the kitchen where I hovered in the doorway. With Matthew and his bike teetering on the precipice of the basement stairs, I deferred to his father's judgment, holding my breath.

"You got this, Matthew," Mike said. "A few more inches and you'll clear the door."

Grunting and sighing heavily, Matthew struggled to maneuver his bike around the tight turn. His face grew red with exertion, his look equal parts determination and defeat. As the drama mounted, I walked away. I couldn't watch.

Moments later, I heard a crash and an angry shriek. I ran to the doorway to see Matthew lying on the concrete basement floor ensnared by his bike, trying to free his legs. Mike ran down, and I followed quickly. Like a cornered animal, Matthew was wild-eyed, his howls a mix of terror and rage. The intensity of the outburst intimidated even Mike, whose tough love melted as he gently untangled his son from the bike. A patch of red grew on Matthew's chin and dripped onto his shirt. I wanted to explode at Mike. *Can't you see what's going on in our family? Matthew can't do these things anymore. I can't do this anymore!*

I would yell at Mike later, I told myself. Now, we had to get Matthew to a doctor to close the gash on his chin.

Three stitches later, we arrived back home. I sat stiffly on our bed. Mike leaned against my dresser, facing me.

"I saw that coming." I shook my head and closed my eyes. "I knew it would end badly."

In a voice equally defensive and defiant, Mike said, "I wouldn't have had him bring his bike down if I thought he was going to get hurt."

I looked at the ceiling, trying to blink back tears. Mike came over to sit next to me and take my hand.

"Karen, Matthew is ten. When is he going to learn?"

When is who *going to learn?*

Two weeks later, Matthew entered fifth grade and Stephen started kindergarden. At five, our second son was the child our firstborn had been at that age—curious, cooperative, a star student. At ten, two years into his ever-evolving symptomatic stew, Matthew was sometimes unrecognizable from his younger self.

That school year was a litany of Matthew's missing papers, books, assignments, homework, lunch boxes, jackets, sneakers, gym shorts, and several times, his orthodontic retainer. If we had found them all, we could have stocked a sale rack at Walmart. Judging by the overstuffed lost-and-found boxes at my elementary school, many kids lose myriad items. But Matthew excelled in the sport of losing things (even more than he excelled in the losing of sports).

Matthew sometimes lost items so thoroughly in a confined space like his bedroom that even Mike and I couldn't find them. A homework paper was there one minute, gone the next. A pen, a report card, a textbook. How could they disappear when Matthew had not left his room with them? Later, we might find the homework paper on the floor of his closet, the pen in his dresser drawer, the textbook tucked in with our income tax binders on the shelf.

Other times, Matthew couldn't find an item in plain sight. I taught him to "look with your hands" as a method of focusing his eyes and his attention. When he entered his room in search of a missing paper, for example, he was to touch his hand on 1) his desk 2) his bed 3) the bookshelf 4) his backpack 5) the floor near his desk. Only then could he come to Mike or me for help.

One night, Mike helped Matthew get organized for homework, making sure he understood the assignment, had the correct page open in his textbook, and all the supplies at his fingertips. Across the hall, I lay on my bed with Stephen, reading to him. When Mike left Matthew's room, I called to him.

"Mike, I'm almost done with this book. I'll check on Matthew after I finish."

"Okay. My blood sugar's getting low. I'm going to the kitchen for a snack."

Five minutes later, I checked on Matthew. He held his head in his hands, fingers tapping his scalp. I rubbed his shoulders, then pointed to the page.

"Is this the question you have to answer?"

"Um, I don't know."

"I heard Dad say, 'Question three.'"

"Oh."

In the calmest voice I could manage, I said, "Matthew, you have to stay focused, otherwise, you'll be here all night."

After talking through question three and its answer, I left to help Stephen brush his teeth. Meanwhile, Mike came back upstairs. I heard him in Matthew's room, his voice strident.

"You're still on question three? What have you been doing all this time?"

Neither Mike nor I ever walked in on a homework session to find Matthew lying on his bed reading comic books, playing with his Game Boy, or engaged in a non-homework activity. We found him in his chair, right where we left him, usually gazing into space, tapping his pencil or fingers, face-scrunching, or wrist-rolling—his newest tic--the *vroom-vroom* gesture kids do to imitate a motorcycle. Was he lost in thought, lost in a fugue state, lost in space? We didn't know, so Mike and I described it to each other simply as "Matthew is lost." I knew what steps to take to look for a missing book, misplaced jacket, or mislaid worksheet, but how does one find a child lost within himself?

The next day, I had Matthew do his homework in the kitchen. As I prepared dinner, I tiptoed around, trying not to make noise. To keep Matthew on task, I used the oven timer, an egg timer, and clocks. To mark his place, I used rulers and paper clips. To keep his eyes focused where they belonged, I cut a narrow rectangular hole in a five-by-eight-inch index card. Placed on a page, the card functioned like a surgical drape around the area of an incision. Still, Matthew lost his place, got confused, forgot what he was doing. I broke his work down into smaller and smaller pieces until the only thing left to break was my temper.

My youngest brother, Mark, visited for a few days that fall and generously offered to help Matthew with homework. Later, he told me, "If I didn't know Matthew was smart, I might think he was...you know...mentally disabled." I wasn't offended because I thought the same thing.

I remembered the end of second grade when Matthew had received an invitation to join the gifted and talented program at school.

"Woo hoo!" I had said, kissing him and hugging him tightly. "Congratulations, Matthew!"

"Way to go, Matthew," Mike said, giving him a high-five.

At the time, I worried Matthew might brag to his friends. Gifted programs were not yet considered elitist and racist, but I thought about little Nathaniel, who struggled in school, and I didn't want Matthew to make him feel bad. I toned down my enthusiasm and said to Matthew, "You know this doesn't mean you're better than anyone else, right?"

Now, with Matthew floundering in fifth grade, I wanted to take it back. "Shout it to the rooftops!" I wanted to tell his younger self. "Don't ever be shy about being smart." I wanted to hug that gangly little boy and never let him go. "Tell everyone you're smart, Matthew," I would say, thinking to myself *because someday you might not be.*

Mike and I made the difficult decision to pull Matthew from the gifted program early in fifth grade. When I told the instructor, she balked. "Matthew is so smart. He has such potential." Did she see the same child we saw at home? At times, Matthew seemed like his old self-quick witted, animated, well-spoken. We called these his "Einstein moments." But the brilliant scientist was usually AWOL when Matthew sat at his desk, swamped with homework, so Mike and I stuck with our decision.

When we talked with Matthew's homeroom teacher about the homework battles, he didn't seem overly concerned, even though he saw the same distractibility and disorganization in school. Matthew's strengths—his well-structured and humorous writing (although his penmanship had become almost illegible), his easy grasp of science concepts, and the rare occasions when he quickly solved math problems—outweighed his weaknesses. And Matthew's cooperative behavior kept him off the "problem" radar in school. I imagined there were a dozen students in the classroom needier than him.

The stress at home showed up in dreams about my students. Although my job was demanding—providing classroom lessons for a school of 500 children, 100 of whom also participated in one or more of my support groups—home life was the hassle. Yet my students, not my children, plagued me in recurring dreams.

> *I'm herding a large group of children from my school through the airport terminal, trying desperately to get them to a particular destination. I hurry up and down escalators, through endless lobbies and long hallways. The horde of kids follows me like lemmings as I sprint through dense crowds. I keep looking over my shoulder, afraid I'll lose my charges, afraid one child will get left behind, so afraid, always afraid. Then we take off in*

another direction. I'm running and running, a mara-
thon with no finish line, a desperate, frenzied, fruitless
rush to some unknown place we never reach.

The dreams came several times a week, lasting for what felt like hours. I awoke headachy, dazed, and disoriented, as if I had worked all night.

Hockey was an albatross. In the learn-to-play years, when kids were five or six, parents got their skaters dressed and strapped into the assorted safety pads, but by the time players were ten, most parents expected them to dress themselves with minimal supervision. Matthew needed maximum supervision, not only because of his distractibility, but because his sensitivity to touch had escalated.

As a newborn, he had often craned his head away from us when we held him, reminding me of autism case studies I'd read as an undergrad. As a preschooler, Matthew became hysterically silly when we cut his toenails; it took both Mike and me to hold him down. Until he was eight, he chewed on the necks and wrists of his clothing. But his reactions in those limited situations paled in comparison to dressing for hockey at age ten.

I often told Matthew to bring his equipment down from his room so he could dress while I fixed dinner. One night, it took him three trips up and down the stairs to get everything he needed. Then he sat on a kitchen chair, lost.

"Matthew, put your shoulder and elbow pads on first."

He positioned and repositioned the pads with sighs and

grunts, finally throwing an elbow pad to the floor.

"I can't get it right!"

I set down the serving spoon in my hand to help him.

"Now see if you can get your jersey over your pads."

After a few tries, he stamped his foot on the floor.

"It doesn't feel right!"

He proceeded to lace and re-lace, buckle and re-buckle, strap and re-strap every piece of equipment on his body, often breaking into a tearful rage.

Sometimes Mike got home in time to help get Matthew ready, but if Mike was running late, I tried to have our hockey player ready to hop in the car as soon as his father got home. If Mike had a meeting or was traveling, it was all on me. Later, I soothed myself with a binge.

"It's not the right sport for Matthew," I complained to Mike. "Can't we just stick to soccer?" Shorts and shin guards—what a breeze. But neither son nor husband wanted out and I lacked the fortitude to force the issue. Plus, after such an expensive investment, I hated to call it quits.

One night, *60 Minutes* aired an episode on OCD—obsessive compulsive disorder. A chronic and long-lasting disorder, OCD is characterized by two types of symptoms: *Obsessions*—unwanted, uncontrollable, and recurring thoughts and fears that drive a person to have *compulsions*—repetitive behaviors that interfere with daily activities, causing significant distress.

In the show, a beautiful blond-haired girl about Matthew's age had multiple common symptoms of OCD. She re-tied her shoes dozens of times a day, washed her hands excessively, and repeated specific phrases every time she left a room. In another case, a young girl valiantly tried to pull on leggings before exploding with agitation. "They bother me!" When her mother gently encouraged her to try other clothing, the girl rolled around on the bed, stomped on the floor, and flung clothing across the room, shrieking and whining. Her mother's stoic look spoke volumes. I knew the effort it took to maintain her cool. I understood if she lost her resolve for even a moment, she would snap. I could easily picture it because I lived on that edge of composure nearly every day. If a film crew came to our house on hockey night, I wondered, would we be their next story?

Despite my feeling of solidarity with the mother, I ruled out OCD for Matthew because he didn't have the classical presentation—fear of dirt and germs, grooming rituals, a need for symmetry, order, and precision. *If only he wanted order,* I thought ruefully. Instead, he was impossible to peg. Often lethargic, spacey, and clumsy, under pressure—as with homework or hockey, or when he was overly tired or hungry—he turned uncontrollably silly and immature. He was rarely uncooperative and never oppositional. In one moment, the positive reports from school—a good grade, a compliment on an assignment—placated me. In the next moment, I'd be back in the middle of a homework session that had dragged on too long, wanting to throw Matthew's book out the window, ask him what was wrong with him, and berate him for being stupid. I wanted to but didn't.

Although, one time I came close.

The evening was unusually warm for October. The smell of burning leaves wafted in through the screen door, and the *thunk* of a basketball dribbled in from down the street. Mike had taken Stephen to run an errand. Matthew sat at a small play table in the kitchen where he and I battled social studies. We had been at it for an hour, and we probably had another hour to go. With every passing minute, Matthew grew more forgetful.

"You already read that sentence, Matthew."

I watched his eyes scanning the pages of his open book, so I held my finger to the correct spot. He drummed his hands on his thighs, scrunched his face, rolled his eyes. Then he got squirmy, sliding in and out of his seat.

"By the count of three, I want your bottom back in that chair."

He kept his bottom in place but slid his feet every which way and waved his arms like a windmill, acting like he was tipsy.

I sat with my arms folded, disciplined and controlled, waiting him out. But my façade began to crack.

In the middle of what happened next, I knew our kitchen lights were a beacon for the darkness outside. If the neighbor behind us stood on his back porch or in the alley, he would witness me at my worst.

In the middle of what happened next, I thought about the times at work I'd been mandated to call child protective services when a student disclosed abuse or neglect. Usually the calls were warranted, but sometimes, good parents got dragged into the system undeservedly. I wondered if tomorrow I'd receive an unwelcome but justified visit from the authorities.

In the middle of what happened next, I knew the potential consequences of my actions, yet I couldn't stop myself.

Without intention or forethought, I jumped up from the table.

"Most parents wouldn't put up with this!" I towered threateningly over Matthew. "Most parents would do *this!*"

I dragged him out of his chair and pushed him to the floor.

He giggled.

"And some parents would do *this!*"

I picked him up roughly, shaking him.

He laughed.

"*This* is what most parents would do!"

I squeezed his arms, scowling at his innocent face before shoving him back into his chair.

As the monster within me took over, the loving mother in me hoped it felt familiar to Matthew. I hoped it felt like we were practicing the abduction-prevention tips taught at school. Parents were supposed to practice, and I'd made a game of it with Matthew and Stephen. I pretended to try to kidnap them, and they practiced going limp or fighting back. In the middle of my tirade in the kitchen, I hoped it felt to Matthew like a game. I hoped, if the neighbor saw, if child protective services came tomorrow, I could tell them it was all just a game.

But it wasn't a game, and it wasn't over.

Matthew rolled off his chair and onto the floor like a giddy drunk, and the monster in me nearly went berserk.

"Some parents would even hurt you or throw you out of the house!"

My voice sounded an octave too high. My arms hung stiffly at my side, fists clenched.

Had Matthew cried or cowered, I would have instantly scooped him into my arms and rocked him and apologized through my tears for hurting or scaring him. But throughout my tirade, Matthew laughed. His affect suggested I hadn't physically hurt him, but I wondered if I was traumatizing him.

Finally, I stormed from the kitchen and took a few deep breaths in the dining room. When my heart stopped pounding, I returned and apologized to Matthew, assuring him that I loved him and would never hurt him on purpose. Matthew didn't seem to care—either that I was out of control or that I was sorry for it. None of it seemed to register.

The incident left me shaken, not so much by what I did, but by what I wanted to do, which was to clobber my child.

The next day, I called Dr. Peterson and asked for a referral to counseling. Matthew and I would go together, regardless of what he or Mike thought. If I wanted to be a better mom, it was about time I did something about it.

I sat on the overstuffed couch in Janis's living room, glass of chardonnay in hand, *Jingle Bell Rock* playing on the stereo. Her home, neighborhood central, was the venue for a mid-December mom's night out. Flitting around the living room, skirting the enormous Christmas tree, Janis refilled wine glasses and replenished chips and dip. I chatted with the other moms, most of whom I liked. One I disliked, not for her stringy gray hair and yellowed teeth swirling in a haze of cigarette smoke, but for her ad-nauseum complaints about her children.

In her mid-forties, the smoker was older than the rest of us, her youngest several grades ahead of Matthew. Known for her troublemaking seventeen-year-old daughter, the mother droned on and on, listing all the things wrong with her child. Smoke poured out of her mouth in gasps, and I tried to hold my breath.

"I don't know what else I can do," she whined.

How about don't be so mean to your daughter, I wanted to say.

Our parenting styles and outlooks were completely different. It wasn't even an apples-to-oranges comparison; it was more like peaches-to-prickly pears. Yet I understood what she meant. I knew what it was like to feel helpless and hopeless with a child.

When the smoker ended her rant, the room grew quiet, thick with the other moms' discomfort. They shifted in their seats, looking awkwardly at each other. Finally, I broke the silence.

"It sounds like your daughter has destroyed your image of what motherhood should be."

Looking at me intently, the smoker took a long drag on her cigarette before turning away. She didn't respond. The other moms quickly resumed their conversations.

My words felt like I'd stuck my tongue to a frozen flagpole and ripped the skin off to disengage. What a horrible thing for me to suggest—that a daughter might cause her mother to resent motherhood, that a child held such power. Most parents could not fathom it, would refuse to believe it.

I could not only fathom it, but I believed it. Intimately. Because it described exactly how I felt about Matthew.

Part 2

10

We Can Hold it, Can't We?

The child psychologist extended his hand. "Call me Adam."

Our appointment had taken months to schedule, but finally, in January 1997, Matthew and I stood on the threshold of a small, windowless office. Three chairs sat across from a desk; one chair sat behind. Against the wall, a bookshelf. The space was otherwise unadorned. Straightforward.

Matthew was in the middle of fifth grade, two-and-a-half-years since the onset of his tics. Mike had come around to the idea of counseling, although the thought of airing one's problems to a stranger made him squirm. His family didn't talk about feelings, even among themselves. Under my influence, Mike had grown more comfortable with touchy-feely conversations, but counseling was still a stretch, and he gladly let me take the reins for our first session.

Matthew and I took our seats across from Adam, who rolled his chair from behind the desk and faced us. The forty-ish doctor in rumpled khakis had wavy brown hair and the widest smile I'd ever seen, just shy of "ear to ear." He bantered with Matthew, who chuckled at references I knew he didn't understand. *You're way over his head*, I tried to communicate telepathically. But I was pleased our counselor made the effort to connect, and I hoped Matthew liked him. I hoped Adam liked both of us.

Relaxing his smile, Adam turned to me.

"So, what brings you here today?"

I expected his question and had prepared my answer. Ours was not simply the story of a troubled child. Ours was a troubled relationship. I didn't bring *Matthew* to counseling. I brought *us*. Yes, Matthew needed help managing his behaviors, and I wanted answers to why he seemed to be falling apart, but I needed help too. I wanted my love for him to override my urge to wallop him. As the adult in the relationship, I needed to take responsibility.

Before I answered Adam, I reached over to give Matthew's knee an affectionate squeeze. I took a deep breath and replied, "I don't have the relationship I want with my son."

Gently, aware of Matthew's presence, I disclosed the homework battles, forgetfulness, and immature silliness. I added my frequent anger and frustration and how it saddened me. Blinking back tears, I said, "I love Matthew with all my heart. I don't want this to be his life. Our life."

Adam leaned back, resting his hands gently on the arms of his chair, legs uncrossed. I recognized it as open body language, and I mirrored his posture. He looked at Matthew.

"Matthew, how does that make you feel?"

"I dunno." Matthew shrugged, rolling his eyes a few times.

After Adam chatted with Matthew, he asked his young client to leave the room and rolled closer to me.

"Are you familiar with ADHD and ADD?"

"I know about ADHD," I said, explaining how I'd dismissed the "hyperactive" label years ago despite Matthew's extreme behavior.

"But he's not as hyper anymore," I added. "His energy has really waned over the past year. And he's not impulsive and never a behavior problem." Straightening my wristwatch without looking at it, I thought about how often Mathew sat at his desk, daydreaming.

"I'm not as familiar with ADD," I said, "but I know it's essentially ADHD without the hyperactivity."

Adam explained the symptoms—daydreaming, lethargy, losing things, difficulty following instructions and organizing tasks or activities. It all fit. ADD described Matthew perfectly.

To test his hypothesis, Adam gave me charts to track troublesome behaviors, guidelines for setting behavioral goals, instructions to devise a family action plan, and assessment sheets for Matthew's teachers and us to complete. I also left with hope. And an idea.

"Mike, I think we should move Stephen into the front bedroom. He's too distracting for Matthew."

At five, Stephen often went to bed as Matthew was trying to concentrate on homework at his desk. The bedtime routine became an interruption. Sometimes Matthew worked downstairs so Mike and I could monitor his progress more easily, but his room needed to be a quiet refuge. Mike agreed, and we presented the plan to the boys.

"Stephen, you'll get the small room all to yourself," Mike

said. "You and Matthew can help me take apart the bunkbeds."

"Matthew, you'll get the big room," I explained. "But Dad is going to move my sewing machine table in there, so sometimes I'll need to use your room." Based on the boys' high-fives and whoops of delight, it seemed to be a win-win.

Matthew was a wrist-rolling, face-scrunching, hip-grinding, tap-tap-tapping whirlwind that year. All the energy from his body fed the tic tempest, leaving the rest of him depleted. His brain a sieve, loose bits of information dripped away, leaving behind a muddle. Yet if others observed the tempest, the depletion, or the muddle, they didn't tell me. Each new symptom such as lethargy or clumsiness wormed its way in so gradually, other adults in Matthew's life didn't notice. Each school year, his new classroom teacher had no way of knowing how or who he used to be. In their eyes, Matthew was a nice kid, quirky and flaky, never a discipline problem, one of many odd but likable students turnstiling through the school year.

My parents observed Matthew's oddities when we visited over the holidays or on school breaks, but they never seemed alarmed. Of course, free from the duress of schoolwork on those visits, Matthew's symptoms were apparent but less problematic. When I called my parents to vent my frustration, they heard only their little girl's distress, making them tone-deaf to the source of my angst.

Mike waffled on his stance. Even after a heartfelt discussion where he appeared to share my worries, the next day, I might overhear him prodding Matthew like a tenacious coach, telling him to try harder and be tougher. Discipline and determination characterized Mike's response to his diabetes. He refused to let it beat him. He wanted that for Matthew, too. He wanted to be a good father, and he succeeded on many levels. Still, he didn't know Matthew like I did.

Mike was less attuned to Matthew's decline for myriad practical reasons. My workday was shorter. Mike dropped the kids off at school in the morning and I picked them up in the afternoon, which meant critical hours of observation happened on my watch. Although Mike helped with homework, baths, and bedtime, for every hour he spent with the kids, I spent two or three or four.

On weekends, Mike corralled Matthew and Stephen for batting and soccer practice in the yard, and he never missed a baseball or hockey game. But his cycling, which occurred mostly on weekends, left me to manage play dates, birthday parties, and outings. And when our old house called, as it did frequently, Mike had to pick up due to his expertise in plumbing, electrical, and carpentry. Again, kid duty fell on me.

Finally, call it mother's intuition, a sixth sense—call it what you will—I had it, and Mike didn't.

I wasn't fully aware of the overall disparities in Mike's and my parenting and household responsibilities. That would have required me to step back from the day-to-day drudgery to get a clear picture, and I was too bogged down to do that. I experienced flashes of resentment, though. They simmered when Mike took three hours to get ready for a four-hour bike ride, chaining me to the kids for most of the day. They flared after we loaded the dishwasher, when Mike said, "We're all done, right?" to which I answered "yes," leaving me to scrub the pans and wipe the counters. What broke my composure, though, was the chaos and clutter that inundated every room in our house.

Mike and I both tolerated a certain level of dust and detritus at home. Lath-exposed walls, unfinished wood trim, and half-stripped wallpaper didn't faze Mike, and I tolerated the mess as long as we made progress. But we often abandoned an indoor project to devote the summer to outdoor tasks, and vice versa. Sports, church, and social obligations whittled away our free time, stalling renovations and repairs for months or years. My patience ran out regularly.

One day, I opened a credit card statement to see that we'd incurred a late fee. Again. We shared bill-paying, a risky liaison in a home with four or more possible places for everything and nothing ever in any of those places.

In search of the overdue bill, I looked upstairs on our disheveled desk, failing to find what I wanted but discovering a permission slip for Matthew due the next day. On my dresser, I spied the checkbook I usually kept in my purse and tucked it under my arm. On Mike's bedside table, partially hidden under a stack of receipts, I found the missing shed key, but no bill. Downstairs in the foyer, I dug through a pile of accumulated mail and finally uncovered the envelope I sought, unopened.

I waited for Mike to get in the door, hang his jacket on the coat rack, and give me a kiss before I pounced.

"Mike, we're late again on our credit card." My tone was intense, scolding, blaming.

"Oh, we are?"

"We have to be better about keeping track of stuff. The late fee is twenty-five bucks."

"Well, we've been so busy."

"I know, but we can't keep letting this happen."

"Karen, we're doing our best."

"We're *so* unorganized! I *hate* that we can never find anything. We should have *one place* for all our important papers." I flapped the bill in the air as I spewed my pent-up anger. I wasn't screaming, but I didn't need to. My acerbic words clearly expressed my emotion.

Mike ran his hand over his face. Wisely, he didn't try to argue or respond further.

"I'm going to take care of this right now," I said through clenched teeth as I marched to the kitchen. Without looking back, I waved the shed key in the air. "And I found *this*. I'll put it in the drawer where it's *supposed* to be."

It ended there. It always ended there, without me articulating a solution or making a request, without Mike having a clear response, without us calmly discussing the issue. When I implored Mike to brainstorm with me how to prevent these repeated scenes, he resisted, and I backed down. When I devised a system, he didn't follow it, and I didn't insist. When he established a method, I rejected and overrode it.

And I wondered why we never seemed to solve our problems.

At our next appointment with Adam, I gave him the completed behavioral rating sheets. Two weeks later, Mike and I sat side-by-side, holding hands. After introductions and updates, Adam held up a stack of paper.

"I studied your responses and those of Matthew's teachers on these questionnaires. I'd like to refer Matthew to our child psychiatrist to be evaluated for ADD."

I looked at Mike. Although my colleagues often recommended psychiatric evaluations for students with behavior difficulties, I never imagined my own child would need one. Mike had probably never heard anyone discuss child psychiatry. He looked glum.

Adam continued. "I think there may be some depression going on, too."

That Matthew might be depressed never occurred to me. But hadn't I told Adam that Matthew rarely wanted to play with friends lately, that he seemed tired all the time? I caught Mike's eye again. We both frowned.

"And Matthew may benefit from a trial of Ritalin."

The stimulant drug was controversial. Some parents and educators swore by its efficacy; others claimed the medication caused a host of side-effects including seizures, heart problems, and personality changes. One side argued that, in addition to academic benefits, children's self-esteem improved when they weren't getting in trouble. The other side insisted that kids were naturally full of energy, and the adult world should adapt to the needs of children, not the other way around. I believed the decision should be made on a case-by-case basis.

I took a deep breath. Mike tightened his grip on my hand.

"We'll talk about the Ritalin," I said, knowing the decision would weigh heavily on us. "And we'll see what the psychiatrist has to say."

After dinner one night, Matthew and Stephen played with Legos behind the living room couch while Mike and I cleaned up the kitchen. The couch sat a few feet from the bay window, creating a quiet, protected space for the boys to build their dreams. I loved that it kept the Lego clutter hidden and out of the path of my bare feet, theoretically, at least.

Except for weekends, Matthew rarely had leisure time to spend in the boy cave. Stephen retreated there often, and I wondered if he did it to escape the tension of his homelife. Not that we had screaming matches, but Mike and I sometimes raised our voices and sounded angry. Was Stephen avoiding that?

I watched him for signs of anxiety—stomachaches, tantrums, separation avoidance, behavioral difficulties-but he never gave me reason to worry. Stephen was easy. His contentment and independence were blessings.

"Hey Matthew," Mike called when we finished in the kitchen, "come sit on the loveseat with Mom and me." We had met with Matthew's fifth grade teacher after school and wanted to give him an update.

I turned on the light and moved a pile of newspapers to the floor. Matthew slogged over in his baggy sweats, his gold wire-rim glasses—a newly discovered need—slightly askew on his face. Mike gave him a side hug, and I kissed him on the forehead.

"We want to tell you about our meeting with Mr. McDonald," I said.

Mike leaned forward, resting his arms on his legs. "We told him how hard you're working at home."

"And we're all proud of you," I said, "because we know you're doing your best."

Matthew's head swiveled back and forth as Mike and I practically tripped over ourselves giving him positive encouragement.

I tucked my hair behind my ears. "Mr. McDonald said Dad and I can cut you off when we think you've done enough homework."

"So, you have to let us do that, okay?" Mike said.

Matthew nodded.

"What do you think about that?" I asked.

"I dunno. Okay, I guess."

We sat for a moment. Mike cleared his throat. "Do you have anything you want us to know, Matthew?"

"Uh-uh."

Most of our conversations with Matthew regarding school-related conferences sounded similar, ending with hugs and kisses and *we love yous*. But did we ever ask Matthew about his waning abilities? Was he aware of the changes inside him? He knew homework was difficult, that his parents got mad at him, that we talked with his teachers. But did he know his skills, his talents, his *Matthew-ness* was slipping away?

I often checked in with Matthew about his feelings, and he seldom had more than an "okay" in response. But Mike and I never sat him down, enfolded him in our arms, and said, *Hey buddy, everything seems so hard for you lately. What do you think is going on?* And if we had, would Matthew have had an answer?

When I was in sixth grade, I could run faster than many of the boys in my class. If someone asked me the next year why the boys now beat me, I wouldn't have had an explanation and would have felt bad being questioned. In the transition from eighth grade in Catholic school to ninth grade in public school, I morphed from outgoing and confident to insecure and reserved but would have lacked the words to say why. In high school, I managed decent grades in math and science early in the year when the material was basic, but when concepts grew complicated, my grades tanked.

Was that why I never asked Matthew to explain his decline-because I couldn't explain mine?

I wanted Matthew to be a kid, to let the adults worry about the whys. It wasn't his job to figure this out. Once again, I returned to what I had learned as a psychology undergrad: it's better not to give too much attention to a behavior because you might unwittingly make it worse.

On the ice that year, Matthew's head whipped around a full second or more after the action whizzed by. On the rare occasions he had control of the puck, he passed it to phantom players. The worst, though, was checking (one of the reasons I didn't like hockey). As a weak player, Matthew made an easy target, getting hit often and going down hard. Mike insisted it was part of the game, that with all his padding, Matthew wouldn't get hurt. But every crash into the boards was a bone-crushing blow to me.

During one game, I watched from the stands of the unheated arena everyone called "freezer park." My muscles stiffened with cold and tensed with anxiety. Bundled up in his green snowsuit, Stephen crouched over the seat next to me, trying to color with his mittens on. Next to him stood Mike. "That's it,

Matthew, go after that puck!"

With a *whomp*, Matthew got brutally checked and fell to the ice. For a moment, the silence was deafening. I froze, straining to see movement. Then, Matthew screamed. "My neck!"

I jumped up, hands instinctively covering my mouth, heart wildly pounding. *His neck. Not his neck!* An image of my quadriplegic son flashed through my mind.

Stepping over Stephen, Mike pushed past me and hurried to the ice. Another father followed him, and, along with the coach, they knelt over the fallen player. The rink was hushed. Stephen stood up, yellow crayon in his mittened hand.

"Mommy, what happened?"

I put my arm around him. "Matthew got hurt."

Within moments, the men helped Matthew get up and skate to the bench.

"Matthew's okay! Let's clap, Stephen." And we did, accompanied by the sound of the players slapping their sticks on the ice.

Mike climbed back to our seats and told me the other father, a doctor, said Matthew's injury was only a strain, and he should sit out the rest of the final period. I fumed—at Mike for pushing this sport, at Matthew for being vulnerable, at the players for being unnecessarily rough, at the other parents for allowing their sons' aggression.

Other moms appeared to take all this in stride—sports, childhood bumps and bruises, the demands of motherhood, even the worrying. I wasn't cut from that cloth. Motherhood was too hard, like trigonometry or physics, and I wanted to quit. Not on my child—I'd never quit on Matthew, but I wanted out of what society expected of us. Like a mama tiger, I wanted to gently pick him up by the scruff of his neck and carry him away to a quiet den where I could guard the entrance and keep him safe.

After another game in which Matthew again seemed as out of place on the ice as a basketball, I stood in the stands near the locker room, waiting for Mike to come out with our tired player. Stephen jumped back and forth on the bleacher steps. The Zamboni circled the ice, leaving mirrored swaths in its wake, rattling the plexiglass as it passed. Sooner than expected, Mike hurried out of the locker room with Matthew trailing behind, still in his full hockey uniform. They both looked tense.

"Mike, what's —"

"Matthew will get changed at home."

"Is everything—"

"I'll explain later."

A quick scan of Matthew showed he was unhurt, so I quelled my curiosity.

"Good game, Matthew," I said as he trundled past me. It was my stock response whether I believed it or not.

At home, Matthew immediately went up to shower, Stephen made a beeline for Saturday cartoons, and Mike took me aside in the kitchen.

"Matthew wet himself during the game," Mike whispered.

"You mean, like, *he peed his pants?*"

"Yeah, he said he couldn't get to the bathroom in time."

We shook our heads at each other, baffled and speechless. Eventually, we convinced ourselves the accident was an anomaly. Then it happened at several more games, and once on a flight to Pittsburgh. I sought the counsel of my expert colleagues. They were familiar with bedwetting at this age but not daytime incontinence. I don't remember talking about it with Adam, but I must have. I imagine him nodding, taking it in, suggesting I tell Matthew's pediatrician.

I did tell Dr. Peterson. She listened as she dried her freshly washed hands on a paper towel. Matthew sat on the table, drumming his legs with his fingers.

"Boys have accidents because they get busy. They wait until the last minute to go to the bathroom. It's normal."

It didn't sound normal to me. Maybe at age five, but not at ten.

Pulling her Mickey Mouse stethoscope from her neck, Dr. Peterson gave a perfunctory listen to Matthew's chest. He giggled and squirmed.

"Matthew, you can hold it if you try, right?"

"Yeah."

What's a ten-year-old boy going to say? "No, I can't hold it. I wet myself like a baby?"

I should have said, in a calm, measured voice, *It seems to me that he can't hold it, or he would have done that.* I should have demanded further investigation—a specialist, a test, a magnifying glass on the problem. But I smiled and let Dr. Peterson believe I concurred.

At that same appointment, I told Dr. Peterson about Adam's ADD theory, about our upcoming psychiatric appointment, and the possible trial of Ritalin.

"Would you like to start him on a temporary low dose now? Then you and the psychiatrist can evaluate its effect?"

Why not? My ten-year-old wet his pants. We're desperate.

The following week, I called her to report eagerly that Matthew's concentration had dramatically improved. A week later, I called again. Matthew's progress had completely deteriorated.

"It's not ADD, then," she concluded brusquely, and I wanted to reach through the phone, yank Mickey from her neck and scream in his ear: *Well then what the hell is it?*

11

Red Herrings

Pinching my earlobes, I felt for both earrings. I tightened my blouse bow, then ran my hand over my hair to calm the flyaways dancing in the dry March air. Perched in a waiting room chair, I imagined the psychiatrist would be white-haired and pompous, peering over his bifocals in judgment.

Absorbed in his Game Boy, Matthew sat next to me, his nylon wind pants making a soft *swish* when he shifted in his seat. Mike didn't join us. With limited vacation and sick leave, we had to conserve our resources. My motto: Divide and conquer. Besides, I talked the talk of child development and mental health, not Mike. I wasn't a clinician like most of my middle and high school counterparts; in fact, I knew little about child psychiatry. My expertise was educational program development and implementation. Still, my crumb of knowledge was a whole pie compared to Mike's empty plate. For him to attend the psychiatry appointment made as much sense as me discussing with an electrician where to place a junction box.

"Matthew?"

A plump, middle-aged woman with red hair and oversized glasses beckoned us, and we followed her—an office assistant, I presumed—into a blue-walled office. When the door closed behind us, she extended her hand and smiled.

"Hello. I'm Dr. Graham."

I almost laughed. *What, no bifocals?*

After introductions, I launched into my well-rehearsed spiel of Matthew's symptoms, including the urinary incontinence and the Ritalin trial and failure. As I talked, Dr. Graham nodded, occasionally scribbling on a notepad.

"Dr. Peterson doesn't think it's ADD," I concluded. "But I'm not willing to give up so easily."

Dr. Graham waved her hand in dismissal, jutted out her chin, and gave me a response I didn't realize I had craved.

"Me neither."

I wanted to wrap my arms around her and kiss her on the cheek. Finally, I had an ally.

She quizzed Matthew about activities and friends, and his answers painted the picture of a life rich in social success. I hated to burst his bubble, but how could this doctor help us unless she knew our reality? After Matthew left for the waiting room, I told Dr. Graham the truth.

"Matthew rarely plays with his peers anymore. He's always so tired or just uninterested. And his friends seem to have forgotten about him." I looked at my hands folded in my lap before looking up again.

Doctor Graham squinted as she looked out of the side of her glasses, adjusting the frames several times. Then she commented, seemingly to the wall.

"Lack of strong attachments to others is a characteristic of schizoid personality disorder."

I didn't know what a schizoid personality was, but I assumed it was related to schizophrenia. I paid it little attention. I knew Dr. Graham didn't mean to imply Matthew had a serious mental illness. She simply wanted to explain a set of behaviors using pre-established criteria, the way a cardiologist might say, "Chest pain is a symptom of a heart attack, but your chest pain is only indigestion." Or a podiatrist might tell you, "An ingrown toenail can indeed be dangerous, but yours is harmless." Dr. Graham's comment was an off-the-cuff remark that didn't warrant further discussion. It completely left my mind when the next topic entered.

"I think Matthew would benefit greatly from a longer trial of Ritalin. A few studies have suggested it may exacerbate tics, but most of the research shows a decrease in uncontrolled motor activity."

I hadn't heard or read about Ritalin's effect on tics. I pursed my lips and checked my earlobes again.

"You'll need to monitor him closely and call me if you see any significant changes."

"Of course, Dr. Graham."

My mind was a sandstorm. I couldn't grab a single intelligible thought.

Matthew and I left with a prescription to restart his Ritalin, a stack of reading materials, and a folder of worksheets: "Five Ways to Organize Your Study Time," "Six Ways to Get Organized at Home," "Planning Your Homework Time to Write a Report." One of the articles described how a child's level of alertness could fluctuate from minute to minute, hour to hour, day to day, and even week to week. This explained Matthew's continuum of functioning from Einstein moments to lost in space.

After discussions with Adam and Dr. Peterson and my conversations with colleagues, one of whom raved about her daughter's progress on the medication, Mike and I decided to move forward with the Ritalin, hoping and praying we made the right choice.

We now had appointments at least every two weeks through the end of the school year. Adam provided emotional support, Dr. Graham monitored Matthew's physiological and behavioral response to medication, and Dr. Peterson kept tabs on our progress.

To my relief, Mike pushed through his initial discomfort with mental health services and attended his fair share of doctor's visits with and without me. He supported every clinical treatment suggestion while holding on to his preferred home remedies of fresh air, exercise, and a go-get-em attitude. Meanwhile, I doubled down on creative strategies to keep Matthew on task with homework, briefing Mike on how to clip the books open or angle the worksheets for maximum visibility. We didn't have much success. Although his tics didn't worsen on the Ritalin, his behaviors didn't improve. Eventually, Dr. Graham recommended weaning Matthew off the medication.

My work calendar showed day after day of crossed-out meetings and canceled classroom lessons, "SICK" filling the boxes. My own whack-a-mole of complaints included sinus infections, upper respiratory infections, migraines, and insomnia. Between sick days and Matthew's appointments, I missed enough work that my principal commented, "You have been out a lot, you know."

I'd always prided myself on my attendance and work ethic. What if I got fired? Not only did we rely on my salary, but at work, I felt accomplished and competent. I couldn't imagine not working. My self-worth depended on it.

Disclosing my frequent illness to Dr. Peterson at Matthew's next appointment, however, sent her off on another tangent.

"Matthew's homework is still a problem," I said. "Although I've been sick a lot, so Mike's been the primary helper."

"Well, of course Matthew is struggling. He's used to having you help him, not his dad."

I didn't even feel like screaming. What would be the point?

Matthew's memory worsened, and when he did remember, his sense of time was completely off. He might talk about yesterday's field trip, which happened a week before. "When Nana and Grandpa were here last week," he might say, when it had been a month since they left. If Matthew called a classmate to borrow a textbook (a frequent affair), the moment he hung up, he couldn't remember the exchange arrangements. I made him call again, then I took over the conversation.

One day, I gave Matthew what I thought was a simple task. "Take this hanger upstairs, put it in your closet, and bring down your laundry basket."

Matthew was taller now, only a few inches shorter than me. We stood almost eye-to-eye in the kitchen, and I watched as he processed my request. He took the hanger I handed him, then held it suspended in the air. He glanced around, then back at me, his face blank. Muscles in his shoulders and arms twitched almost imperceptibly.

"Put the hanger in your closet."

He nodded.

"Then bring down your laundry basket so I can wash your clothes."

He nodded and headed toward the stairs. Ten minutes later, he hadn't returned. I called up to him.

"Matthew, bring down your laundry basket."

When he came down, I asked, "Did you put the hanger away?"

With complete innocence, he said, "What hanger?"

On another day, Matthew had finished homework in the kitchen, and as he gathered his materials, I held out his school fundraising envelope.

"Matthew, here's our candy order. Put it in your backpack with your homework so you don't lose it."

He held a book in one hand and a pencil in the other. For a few seconds, he reached out his laden hands one at a time to me but couldn't figure out how to take the slip of paper. Three items were too much for his two hands. He looked around for a place to set the book or pencil.

"Uh. Um," he repeated, until, finally, with a helpless shrug, he gave me the book, and I took it, feeling equally helpless.

When he got frustrated, Matthew struggled to express himself. "Uh, um, uuuuh..." Eyes rolling, face scrunching, he craned his head back and flopped his hands around on his thighs, searching for a word or feeling. I got in the bad habit of finishing his thoughts for him. "Is that what you mean, Matthew?" Usually, I was right.

But I wanted to help Matthew communicate better. When he seemed at a loss, I now told him, "Use more words." It became my mantra, helping him to slow down and think through his thoughts, helping me to slow down and let him.

One morning at work, before students arrived for the day, I stopped by a classroom to say hi to Lucy, one of my few confidantes at school. An experienced and compassionate third-grade teacher, Lucy sat folded into a pint-sized chair at a low table, nibbling Triscuits. I plopped down, declining the box she held out to me. Outside, school buses idled, their diesel fumes wafting in through the windows, and Lucy and I blinked back the irritation.

She asked about Matthew, and I explained the counseling, the psychiatry appointment, the ongoing peculiar behaviors.

"And what about you?" she asked, pushing her black bangs from her forehead. She knew I'd been sick because I'd twice canceled my classroom lessons with her students.

"I have another sinus infection. And now the Nyquil that used to knock me out seems to keep me awake. I barely slept last night."

"Could you be depressed?" Her tone was conversational, without judgment.

"I don't know." I tapped my finger on my lips. "I never thought about it."

"I only ask, Karen, because frequent illness is a symptom of depression."

Then the morning bell clanged, and Lucy hurried off before

I had time to reply. Bewildered, I left her sunny classroom for my basement office. Wouldn't I know if I was depressed? I was a counselor, after all. But I didn't mope around looking sad, and I'd never been unable to get out of bed. I did cry—often, now that I thought about it—but I was stressed, not depressed. I loved my job, I loved my husband. Matthew had some problems, but I loved my kids. I was in counseling and a support group, but I wasn't depressed.

Was I?

"Could I be depressed?" I asked my support group. I described the intensity of my food binges, frequent colds and sinus infections, poor sleep, frustration with Mike, hopelessness about Matthew.

"That sounds like a lot of pain," a member responded.

"Could I be depressed?" I asked my primary care doctor. I explained that I woke every night at three a.m. and couldn't get back to sleep.

"Sleep problems have nothing to do with depression," she said.

"Could I be depressed?" I asked my new therapist. I admitted to crying often but didn't tell her about the numerous times I holed up in the bathroom, running the water and exhaust fan to mask my noise. I didn't mention how often I cried in bed after Mike went to sleep or in my car after work, wiping my tear-stained face before I got home.

My therapist recommended I be evaluated by a psychiatrist. As I waited for an appointment, I wondered how I would survive another eight years until Matthew went away to college. *How would I survive another week?*

By the day of my psychiatry appointment, I had read up on

depression and became convinced the diagnosis fit. As soon as I got comfortable in the drab, dimly lit office, practically the moment the slightly built man in corduroys and a cliché tweed jacket clicked open his pen, I began to heave and sob. For a few minutes, I could barely get out a word. When I finally described what was going on with Matthew and my physical and emotional ailments, the psychiatrist made his assessment quickly and prescribed an antidepressant.

"It may take six weeks for you to notice a difference," he cautioned.

It seemed like a lifetime.

In the meantime, self-medicated with ibuprofen, decongestants, coffee, and sugar, I plastered a smile on my face and faked my way through each day. Behind closed doors at home, I had regular meltdowns. When I let Mike witness my more moderate displays of emotion, he looked confused and concerned as he stroked my hand or patted my back. He understood dripping faucets and leaky pipes, not the periodic gushing from my eyes.

"Feel better now?" he asked with loving concern in the calm that followed.

"Yes," I lied, magnifying my suffering.

I kept the worst cries to myself. Mine was an ugly, raw, lacerating grief that I only felt as deeply as I needed when no one was around to watch. It would be too scary for Mike. It was almost too scary for me.

God was watching, I knew, and I beseeched the ceiling for His help, but I didn't know what, exactly, to request. I never believed in asking God to fix things. Since childhood, I always had this sense that others' trials and tribulations were worse than mine. As if there were a heavenly cap on miracles, I felt it was selfish to ask God to dissolve my troubles. I believed His role was to provide strength and hope, so I prayed for strength to survive the next day and hope that things would get better. But I felt abandoned by God. Where was He?

One particularly bad night, I escaped after dinner to the upstairs bathroom and ended up on the floor, curled into a ball. I didn't want to get up. Ever. I felt trapped with no strength left. No out, no escape, no hope. Life would be like this forever— every day a series of mishaps and crises and frustrations and exhaustion. Nothing ever changed and nothing *would* change.

Reaching for a tissue, I saw my pink disposable razor on the edge of the tub. I sat up and stared at it. Picking it up, I felt its weight in my hand. It was a Daisy, my favorite brand, the kind with the thin white Teflon strip to reduce irritation. *Reduce irritation—ha.* Turning it over, back and forth in my hand, I looked at it for… how long? I removed the protective cover. *Protective.* I placed the cover on the tub. I looked at the blades starting to rust, side-by-side dual blades for a smooth finish. *Finish.*

I thought about stories of people who slit their wrists. People who survived because they cut across their wrists. Others who sadly didn't survive because they cut lengthwise up their arms.

What would drive someone to do that? How bad does it get before you reach that point?

I didn't know the answer. Or did I?

Bringing the razor to my wrist, for a moment, I held it there.

Gently, I drew the blades across my skin. Not hard enough to cut. Just enough to leave a tiny white scratch on the surface of my mottled flesh. It was so light, it disappeared as I watched.

So this is how it feels. This is what it's like when it gets so bad, you want to end it.

Now, I understood.

Yet, I knew I didn't want to die. I *couldn't* die. If I did, who would fight for Matthew? I knew what people would say:

Ah. That was the problem all along. Suicidal mother.

Must have been severely depressed. No wonder the son had problems.

She claimed he was falling apart, but it was her the whole time.

The Daisy could not be my out. Another mother might choose the razor blade, but for me it wasn't a choice. Another way *had* to exist. I had to find it or invent it, and I couldn't quit until Matthew was better.

I replaced the protective cover and tossed the pink plastic in the trash, making a mental note to add razors to my shopping list.

My puffy eyes, red face, and smeared mascara stared back at me from the mirror. I fixed my face as best I could, smoothed my hair and straightened my clothes. I checked my wrist. Not a clue remained. With a deep breath, I left the bathroom and turned off the light as I headed to the kitchen. Matthew was sure to be needing me.

I told no one about that night—not Mike, my psychiatrist, therapist, or support group. If others knew, the problem of Matthew's decline would disappear in a sea of confusion, my pink razor blade the red herring leading everyone astray.

12

Forgetting Birthday Cupcakes

Our family foursome shivered on a sports field waiting for Matthew's track meet to begin. Stephen, five, pretended to throw a shot put, imitating a group of boys across the lawn. Mike and I smiled at each other.

"Stephen, do you want to join track when you're old enough?" Mike asked.

"I'm gonna throw that ball all the way over everyone's head."

"It's called a shot put." Mike smiled, bending down to correct Stephen's form.

Like Matthew, some of the kids were bundled in jackets and knit hats. Others in muscle shirts and shorts jogged in place, puffs of condensed air escaping their mouths. Parents, sipping from steaming cups, tiptoed around ice-encrusted patches of mud.

My colleague, Tom, had started the club and asked me if Matthew might like to join. Mike and I were giddy with optimism. Despite Matthew's agile, lanky limbs being replaced by hefty, clumsier versions, despite our gazelle no longer leaping, we believed he would finally discover his athletic niche. Forget the aggression and cumbersome equipment of hockey. Forget the pinball action of soccer. Throw on a muscle shirt and a pair of sneakers and watch him fly.

Matthew didn't share our enthusiasm, but in his usual eager-to-please fashion, he agreed to give it a try.

On a warm-up lap around the track, Matthew lagged behind the other runners, and as the stragglers came around the far bend, he kept eyeing the sidelines as if he wanted to collapse there. For the 100-meter dash—his first event—it looked as if he ran through pudding that sucked at his body from behind, fighting his forward motion. With a look of fierce determination on his sweat-streaked face, he pumped his legs, yet they barely propelled him.

As he ran, or tried to, Matthew's arms and hands splayed outward as if he held a jump rope. I'd noticed lately that when Matthew stood with his arms hanging at his side, they had a pronounced bend at the elbows. I'd seen the same bend in the arms of stroke survivors and kids with cerebral palsy. The word that came to me was *foreshortening*. Plus, the way Matthew ran with his hands angled out looked like some kind of *spasticity*. I didn't completely understand the terminologies or what the postures implied, but a feeling of dread came over me.

Mike and I watched in shocked silence. After the first race, Mike took Matthew aside to coach him to close his fists and pump his arms, but Matthew couldn't. The second race was as bad as the first. Matthew was the slowest runner by a lot. Embarrassingly slow—for us and, more importantly, for him.

In the long jump, Matthew struggled to clear even a couple of feet. Afterward, in a rare reflection on his waning abilities, he complained to me.

"Mom, I jumped further than that last year in gym class."

"I know, buddy," I said, rubbing his back. "I know." *What else could I say?*

"Something is really wrong," Mike confided to me later at home. I didn't ask why the track fiasco stood out as his defining moment. Maybe it killed his dream of a fast-footed son. Maybe it spoiled his enjoyment of the sport. Maybe it threatened to break the father-son bond.

"I agree," I said, with extreme restraint. What I wanted to yell was *That's what I've been trying to tell you!* While I hurt for the pained expression on Mike's face, I was grateful his pain woke him to my reality.

I suggested we try to get Matthew's gym records of his long-jump from the previous year. That would give us quantitative proof of his decline to bring to Dr. Peterson. But when I spoke to the gym teacher and the school secretary, both said the records weren't available.

Then I remembered an old videotape of a backyard Easter egg hunt we'd had toward the end of Matthew's horrible fours. I remembered him being so hyper that day, and I wondered if it would help paint a before picture. Mike watched it with me. Neighborhood kids in their puffy winter coats ran over the bare, winter-parched grass. They scrambled over the swing set, up and down the deck stairs, screaming with delight. When an older child found an egg, he quickly dropped it into his basket and moved on, while the younger children held up their prizes. "Mommy, look!"

At first glance, all the kids seemed to be purposeful in their searches. But then we homed in on Matthew. He ran around the yard helter-skelter, chasing every boisterous exclamation, never hunting on his own. He ended up without a single egg in his basket. Even the three-year-olds had more to show for their efforts. Mike and I laughed at Matthew's spindly-legged energy, but we shared our bewilderment that such a simple game proved so hard for our bright child. My heart broke for Matthew, not because he didn't find any eggs, but because he couldn't.

Would the video help my cause—contrasting younger Matthew's energy with his current lethargy? Or would it hurt us—proving that he'd always struggled to stay on task? I decided not to mention it to Dr. Peterson. The video showed nothing she didn't already know and hadn't already dismissed. My only ammunition was my verbal accounting of his meet.

"Matthew could barely run around the track," I told Dr. Peterson at our next appointment. "His long jump was only a fraction of what it had been the year before."

"He's heavier now," she said. "He can't carry his weight as far."

When I mentioned Matthew's arm "foreshortening" and his "spasticity," she didn't even try to reply. A "harrumph" was all I got.

Dr. Peterson disregarded every complaint I presented.

Me: Matthew trips and falls a lot. He's always getting hurt.

Her: That's preadolescence. All kids go through that clumsy phase.

Me: Matthew's always been so thin but now he's filling out a little too much.

Her: He's finally catching up with the growth curve.

Me: Matthew used to be hyper but now he seems almost sluggish.

Her: Of course. He's putting on weight. What would you expect?

I pushed. She pushed back. I retreated. Even if I had the skill and fortitude to counter her, I knew everything she said was true. I saw the clumsy phases and weight gains in the kids at my own school. I saw the personality changes. All those hormones kicking in before their teenage years, and those fifth graders were different people than they had been a year before. Every symptom Matthew experienced fell within the normal range of preadolescent behavior. Well, then, what was my argument?

"It's not normal *for Matthew*" was my argument. When I said that to Dr. Peterson, finally articulating what I had felt in my bones, she relented and gave me a script for lab work. I took Matthew the next day, and he never complained or expressed nervousness. But he passed out—a "vasovagal response" according to the phlebotomist, caused by a sudden drop in blood pressure due to emotional stress, the sight of blood, or actual or anticipated pain. I hated subjecting Matthew to that trauma. I hated that he suffered. I hated that he tried to be brave and the world repaid him with more obstacles to overcome.

And it was all for naught because the blood work came back negative.

Meaning—what? Nothing was wrong? *I* was wrong?

Toward the end of the school year, Mike and I took Matthew to sixth grade orientation at the middle school. Seated at a long table in the cafeteria, its surfaces scrubbed and gleaming, we nodded and waved to friends and neighbors. "Matthew, there's Danny." I pointed across the room. "Do you want to go say hi?"

He didn't, but instead crossed his arms on the table and rested his head there. I nudged him to sit up when the principal stepped up to the podium. She welcomed us and introduced staff members, while occasional whispers and cracking gum rippled through the room. When she talked about sixth graders changing classes and using lockers, Mike and I shared uneasy looks, despite her assurances that teachers were understanding of students' confusion early in the year. I pictured Matthew still confused in December, racking up detention slips.

I glanced at Matthew slumped over on the bench, eyes glazed. This was too much information for him, took too much energy from him. Periodically, he face-scrunched and *vroom-vroomed* his wrists.

He'll be shark bait.

After orientation, Mike and I agreed that Matthew's only hope for success in middle school was our getting him extra support. That meant having him evaluated for special education services. The topic had come up in our discussions with Adam and Dr. Graham, but Mike and I had hoped to avoid that route. I didn't want Matthew to be teased or ostracized, and I didn't want to admit how far he had declined.

From my training and background, I knew that children thrive when teaching is tailored to their needs. In my school, teachers treated their students who had physical, emotional, or learning disabilities with respect and caring, helping each child to discover their own unique gifts. Beyond the four walls of a classroom, however, society was not always as accepting. Kids with differences of any type drew unwanted attention from their peers. Students who received special education services were often referred to as "labeled." Many parents at the time fought against labeling for their children, judging it to be the school system's scarlet letter.

As a senior in college, I'd taken a course called Abnormal Psychology. My textbook presented cases of children with debilitating autism and adults with severe mental illnesses like multiple personality disorder (later called dissociative identity disorder). I realized how insulting the term "abnormal" was, and I would never use it to describe Matthew. The words *special education* produced a similar sting.

However, I knew that being labeled might also open doors to help Matthew, and whatever the label or lack thereof, Mike and I had always encouraged our boys to use their gifts to the fullest.

I called the school district to start the process.

Soon after, I ate lunch with one of the special education teachers at my school. A circular fan rippled papers on Sue's desk, and she crunched her celery stick as I told her about the middle school orientation and our concerns. She listened, pulling her auburn hair into a ponytail. Then she pointed a long, red fingernail at me.

"Karen, La Salle would love Matthew."

Sue's twins had attended La Salle Institute, a local Catholic military boy's school. The very idea of an all-male military institution sounded rigid and snobby to me, so I never imagined sending my sons there. "It gives me the heebie-jeebies," I told my friends. Sue, however, had always spoken highly of La Salle, describing it as a safe haven for her boys during her divorce.

I pictured the Christian Brothers enfolding my quirky child in a loving, protective cocoon, and my mind cracked open to the possibility.

"Omigod, you're right." I paused with my yogurt spoon poised halfway to my mouth. "And Matthew would love La Salle." Rules and routine. Serious students. Little tolerance of disruptive behavior.

"But Sue, what about the special ed testing?"

"Continue it. Your school district must provide services, even if Matthew goes to private school."

Mike liked the La Salle idea. It was a financial stretch for us, but worth every penny if Matthew grew to be happy and successful. I called La Salle the next day to schedule an admissions interview.

At our next appointment with Adam, Matthew needed my prodding to remember the track meet and middle school orientation. After sending Matthew to the waiting room, Adam listened as I waxed and waned about the negative blood tests, the special ed evaluation, and La Salle.

I shrugged. "Dr. Peterson still believes what's going on is no big deal."

Adam listened, his elbows resting on the arms of his chair, his hands folded in front of his face. Holding my gaze, he rubbed his forehead.

"Karen, something more than ADD is going on with Matthew."

I shifted uncomfortably in my seat. Adam leaned forward to continue, his tone intense.

"I don't know what's happening in his body, but something isn't right."

He paused as I reached for the box of tissues.

"I'll go to bat for you, Karen. I've given Dr. Peterson my assessment, but I can't do it alone. You're Matthew's mom. You're going to have to fight for answers."

For a therapist to give advice is unusual. Therapy is meant to empower clients to make their own decisions as part of the personal growth process. A therapist who gives advice risks robbing his client of crucial insight and learning. When a client's safety is at risk, a therapist may try to help her arrive at a safe course of action. If the client's denial is immutable and their blinders occlusive, however, a therapist may have no choice but to advise. *Call a domestic abuse hotline and don't go home.* Or, *Your risk-taking is endangering your life.* Or, in my case, *You have to fight for your child.*

I wondered how long Adam had been guiding me toward the need to battle, hoping I'd hear a wake-up reveille. Maybe he had dropped breadcrumbs for weeks or months, but I hadn't seen them through my fog of self-doubt.

Sitting back, Adam watched for a moment as I dabbed my

eyes. Then he leaned forward again as if to say something. He rubbed the back of his neck, opened his mouth, then closed it. When he looked at me, he saw right through my defenses.

"No one else will do it for you, Karen."

Clearly Adam had figured out that I wasn't a fighter, that I preferred to have someone else—meaning Mike—do the dirty work. But Adam had also discerned that my husband would not carry the torch.

When I left to gather my wits and retrieve Matthew, internally, I puffed out my chest, determined to heed Adam's call to action.

"Ready, Matthew?"

His fingers paused on his Game Boy, and he looked up at me with trust in his eyes. My chest deflated. I had betrayed Matthew's trust by not listening to what I knew in my heart all along—his deterioration was not normal.

The next day, I called Dr. Peterson and asked for referrals to an OT (occupational therapist) and PT (physical therapist), a route my colleagues had suggested. "Insurance won't cover it," Dr. Peterson replied. *I'll pay for it myself,* I thought.

Then I asked for a referral to a neurologist, and she finally relented.

"I think you need this for your peace of mind."

In other words, Matthew's symptoms weren't the problem—I was.

Matthew's year-end school activities included his snare drum solo in the band concert. He had asked to join the fledgling program, and we thought it would be good for him, a break from the grind of schoolwork. The night of the performance, Mike and I gathered with a smaller and quieter crowd of parents than usual in the cafetorium, since the band had only about fifteen members. The motley group on stage squeaked and squawked through their musical numbers. Then Matthew emerged from the back row in his black dress pants and red, green, and blue block-print shirt. Tripping over a few chair legs, he carried his music stand to the front, then repeated the bumbling as he set up his snare drum. Once in position, he adjusted the snares and fussed with his music. The growing restlessness in the audience made me cringe.

Eyes focused, sticks raised, Matthew awaited the maestro's signal. Suddenly, *brat-a-tat-tat*. His sticks were a blur. *Brat-tat-de-dat*. His wrists flexed in perfect rhythm. *Brat-a-tat-tat-a-tat-tat-a-tat-tat*. His drum roll was a train barreling down the tracks. All the kinetic energy from his body and the fleeting thoughts swirling around his head channeled through his wrists to his hands and fingers. You'd never believe his mind wasn't as sharply tuned as a baby grand, his body as controlled as a conductor's baton. The flare of Matthew's former brilliance kept Mike and I on the edge of our seats for his two-minute solo and sustained our hope for weeks that maybe, just maybe, Einstein lived on.

Stephen's sixth birthday fell on June 24, the last day of school. I baked cupcakes for him to bring and another batch for Matthew's class to celebrate his summer birthday. The following day, at a neighbor's birthday party, we crowded into the living room, the air thick with the smell of sticky, sweet frosting. My neighbor Janis sat across from me, and our four kids sat around us on the hardwood floor. When the hostess passed me a tray of chocolate-frosted confections, I offered it first to Matthew, who sat cross-legged at my feet.

"Boy, Matthew, you get cupcakes two days in a row!"

Janis watched the conversation with a smile, no doubt ready to kid Matthew about all the desserts. But Matthew gave me a funny look, his face blank. I tried to jog his memory.

"Yesterday, you brought in treats for your summer birthday. Remember?"

Licking chocolate from his fingers, Matthew said with complete innocence, "I don't remember anything about any cupcakes."

My eyes gravitated to Janis's face. Her expression matched mine. Mother to mother, woman to woman, we shared a moment of confusion and dread, telegraphing to each other: *How can a kid forget his own birthday cupcakes?*

13

Waiting for Answers

The family outing was Mike's idea. We loaded the kids and an assortment of wheels into the car and drove to a local bike trail. I walked, Mike cycled, Stephen pedaled his two-wheeler with training wheels, and Matthew weaved and lurched ahead of us on rollerblades. Although I'd cringed at the thought of our accident-prone child balanced on rows of spinning disks, I relented like always when Mike presented his plan.

With school out and our homework battles suspended for the summer, family life was relatively peaceful. The OT and PT evaluations I paid for out of pocket revealed no actionable strength, flexibility, or coordination deficits. The PT wrote: "He's just a little clumsy. Reminds me of my own son."

Meanwhile, I sweet-talked myself into believing that whatever was wrong with Matthew—and clearly *something* was wrong—was not serious, that his difficulties would resolve as soon as we identified the culprit. A vitamin deficiency. A hormonal imbalance. An allergy. "I believe there's a magic pill," I told my sister. I didn't mean it literally, though. I didn't think one medication alone would cure Matthew, but I *knew* a definitive answer, a concrete treatment, or a protocol existed to return him to the bright, active child he had been. Or at least get him close.

I believed the magic would happen at our neurology appointment in September, the earliest date available. It seemed light years away, but no amount of pestering on my part—and I did pester—budged either the neurologist's office or Dr. Peterson to move it up.

With no choice but to bide our time, we pretended to be a regular family doing regular family things, like spending the evening at the bike trail.

As we walked, rode, and rollerbladed, a refreshing breeze swept puffs of dandelion seeds across our path and stirred distant trees to dance along. Wildflowers decorated the borders of the crowded blacktop. I couldn't enjoy the scenery, though. I felt on edge watching Matthew's wobbly, erratic movements.

We had just passed a young couple pulling a toddler in a red wagon when the inevitable fall came. Matthew careened forward, landed on his hands and knees, and rolled onto his bottom, screaming like a felled beast. People around us gawked. Although well-protected with pads and a helmet, Matthew reacted like he'd snapped a femur or severed a finger. He clawed at his skates, trying to pull them off. He tore at the straps of his helmet. When he couldn't escape his confinement, he raged, deep throaty roars.

When Mike and I finally freed Matthew, we checked his

scrapes and bruises, none of which looked serious. We gathered him up, turned the bikes around, and dragged ourselves back to our car. On the ride home, my head imploded with all the nasty things I wanted to yell at Mike, but he alone was not to blame. I had been complicit in the decision to let Matthew rollerblade.

"As soon as we get home," I called to Matthew in the back seat, "we'll get you all cleaned up."

"Yeah, you'll be fine," Mike said.

"Anyone want a popsicle before bed?"

"I want grape!" Stephen called.

Matthew stared out the window.

I closed my eyes, dreaming of the bottle of chardonnay we didn't have at home. In my mind, I drank glass after glass, the sharp sweetness deadening my brain until I fell asleep on the couch and woke when our nightmare was over. Then I pictured the batch of peanut butter cookie dough I wouldn't make that I'd never eat in front of Mike anyway. Huddled over the mixing bowl like a child protecting a favorite toy, I'd scoop into the gooey goodness, sucking the sweetness into my mouth over and over until I was numb. Our home didn't have a safe room, either, but I imagined how good it would feel for Matthew and me to lock ourselves in, away from expectations, protected from the world.

Home didn't have what I wanted or needed to soothe my pain. Instead, after Mike and I fussed over Matthew and doled out popsicles, I went to bed early, my only escape, stuck again in inertia.

For the rest of the summer, I didn't push Matthew to ride his bike, play in the yard, or call friends. He became overheated easily, so I let him stay inside in front of the window air conditioner. I expected very few chores from him. Simply getting out the vacuum cleaner tired him, and after a few passes across the carpet, his pale, sweaty face showed he was spent. His lethargy was complete to the point that it oozed out of him and into me.

Over the previous eight months, as Matthew's decline accelerated, I had begun to grasp what it felt like to live in his body. I felt his confinement, his need for space and air. I felt the clothes rubbing the wrong way on his skin, either too tight or so loose they barely brushed the hair on his arms and legs, tickling and teasing. I felt the need for his muscles to twitch, the neurons unable to cease firing. I felt his body's constant, fruitless search for realignment to the perfect position so it could finally, simply relax.

In August, during a family visit to Pittsburgh, my parents took us to Rita's Italian Ice, their favorite summertime haunt. The six of us crammed into my dad's two-door Oldsmobile and arrived at Rita's fifteen minutes later without incident. We sat around a picnic table enjoying our icy desserts as the sky changed from raspberry to blueberry to root beer. Then we piled back in for the ride home.

Mike and Stephen sat in the front bench seat with my dad. Matthew sat in the middle of the backseat between my mother and me. Soon, he squirmed with an unusual urgency. With heavy sighs and loud tongue clicks, he adjusted and readjusted his position and his seatbelt. I wished my dad would stop the car and let Matthew move up front, but he didn't. I said nothing.

I prayed Matthew would calm down for the short ride, knowing he wouldn't, but I was weary of being the only one to speak up on his behalf while the rest of the world watched.

"It's too crowded in here!" Matthew blurted.

"I'll give you more room, Matthew." I squeezed myself against the car door.

My mother sat next to Matthew on the other side, but she didn't react. *Does no one else hear his anxiety? Can't someone acknowledge what's happening?* Matthew's agitation increased. His breathing grew heavy.

"There's not enough room!"

"Here, honey." I pulled gently at his knees. "Put your feet over here. There's lots of room." Moving my feet to the door frame, I cleared the whole floor on my side. He spread out his legs but continued to fidget. Had I been in the front seat, I would have gladly switched with Matthew. I would have lain in the trunk or flattened myself on the roof. But I was stuck in the back with him, helpless and worn. I couldn't make myself any smaller.

No assistance came from the front seat, where Mike and my dad were deep in conversation. *What would happen if I did nothing?*

"I have to get out!"

"We're almost home," Mike and my dad called simultaneously.

Now that Matthew was almost hysterical, he finally had everyone's attention. My mom gently stroked his face. "Deep breaths, Matthew, take deep breaths. Just calm down."

Pull over and let the poor kid out, I screamed in my head. But I couldn't speak. I looked out the window, wishing to be swallowed by the darkening sky.

"I have to get out!" Matthew thrashed like a caged animal. He leaned forward, pulling at the front seat, his neck strained and taut.

His voiced raised an octave. "I can't breathe!"

Enough!

"STOP the car, Dad. Pull over. NOW!"

My dad pulled over quickly. Matthew continued writhing and wailing as my dad got out, Mike got out, then Stephen moved over so the seat could be pushed forward. I stumbled out as fast as I could and finally, finally, finally, Matthew escaped. Gulping in the cool night air outside the confines of the car, he calmed down quickly.

"That's it, Matthew, take deep breaths." I rubbed his back. "How about stretching out your arms? Do you want to run in place a little?"

Mike ran around to my side, and we shared looks of dismay under the streetlight.

"You okay now?" Mike asked as he patted Matthew's shoulder.

"I'm sorry, Matthew," my dad said, looking confused. "I didn't realize you were so uncomfortable."

I'd rarely seen my father cowed and apologetic. He looked vulnerable, and I wanted to yell at him again. In a flash of anger, our relationship experienced a subtle shift. I had become less his little girl and more Matthew's mom.

When Matthew was ready, we all got back into the car, Matthew in front this time, next to the open window, where he sat peacefully for the last two blocks home.

At my parents' house, my mom took me aside.

"Karen, do you know what just happened?"

I didn't. I shook my head.

"That was a panic attack. Matthew just had a panic attack."

Of course. Why hadn't I figured that out? My mother had named it, and it explained not only the car incident, but the rollerblading accident and the fall down the basement stairs the previous summer. Panic attacks. Add one more woe to Matthew's long list of troubles.

The following week, I had a rare moment of solitude at my kitchen table, my after-dinner companions the remnants of grilled chicken and the usual clutter of junk mail and bills to be sorted. Mike had run to a meeting. Matthew and Stephen played out back on the swing set.

The free moments alone gave me the opportunity to escape into the current issue of *Good Housekeeping*, one of my favorite indulgences. I lost myself in a world of "Easy Kitchen Makeovers," "Hardy Perennials," and "Fashion Tips to Look 10 Pounds Thinner." I also read inspiring articles about people who confronted challenges and overcame obstacles. Especially compelling were the tragic stories of families who faced the catastrophic illness or death of a child. I tried to grasp how a mother coped, feeling lucky not to be her, feeling blessed to have two healthy children, my concerns about Matthew momentarily banished.

The current *Good Housekeeping* issue contained such a story, about a family whose six-year-old son had died from a rare genetic disorder. His doctors took a while to arrive at the correct but devastating diagnosis of ALD, or adrenoleukodystrophy, for which no cure existed. Scene by scene, the drama unfolding on the pages collided with my reality.

Little John had been a bright boy before he regressed. His parents called him their "Little Einstein."

Just like Matthew.

John's first symptoms were difficulty paying attention in school and wobbly handwriting.

Just like Matthew.

John was mistakenly diagnosed with attention deficit disorder and prescribed Ritalin.

Just like Matthew.

Then came panic attacks and memory loss.

Just.

Like.

Matthew.

Finally, six-year-old John didn't even know his own name. He survived less than a year.

My head became too heavy to hold up, and I laid it down on top of the open magazine. Squeezing my eyes shut, I tried to barricade out the terrible words I'd read, and I grasped at a truth: *Matthew knows his name.*

Closing the magazine, I skulked over to the pantry where my feeding frenzy began. I scarfed down a package of Little Debbie Swiss Rolls and one of Zebra Cakes, licking the frosting from each cellophane wrapper. Next, a chocolate-covered chewy granola bar, then a second and a third. Grabbing a spoon from the drawer, I dipped and double-dipped super chunky peanut butter. I wanted boxes of oatmeal raisin cookies and a can of chocolate frosting and trays of sweet granola like my mom used to make, and a piece of carrot cake—no—the whole cake, with an inch of cream cheese frosting. Closing my eyes to imagine the feast, I saw the face of little John, John who forgot his name, John with the fatal disease that sounded like leukemia. John who seemed so much like Matthew.

The carbs and fat worked their magic, quieting my storm of emotion. Bloated and lethargic, my mind fuzzy, I felt emotionally sedated and able to function. I had dishes to clean, clothes to get out of the dryer, kids to get ready for bed.

I didn't utter a word to Mike that night about the *Good Housekeeping* article. Nor did I mention it the next day or the day after. I wanted to cradle it for a while, decide how to think about it, imagine saying the words, envision the scene where I opened Pandora's box. The risk was calculated. I had to be careful not to cry wolf and lose what little support I had garnered.

Leukodystrophy remained my secret for several weeks, tucked inside a protective shell of denial and terror. Within the shell, my fears were fiction, untruths I could dismiss.

A week later, on the soccer field, the ball whizzed past Matthew, who reacted eternities later with a look of surprise, like, *Where did that come from?* When the other players huddled together before and after a play, Matthew stood alone, lost. His teammates wore looks of disgust and condescension. They rolled their eyes. I wanted to wag my finger, to make them apologize.

In casual conversations with parents, I made a point to acknowledge Matthew's shortcomings. "My son is not a strong player, as you probably noticed. But he tries so hard and loves to play." I'd laugh to remind them it was only a game. When parents yelled out or mumbled under their breath about a bad play, I cringed, waiting for anyone to criticize Matthew, ready to jump down their throats if they so much as hinted at my child's poor abilities, knowing I lacked the nerve to even ask them politely to tone it down.

The only person who openly complained was Mike. He wasn't the type of father who belittled any player, including his own son, and he'd never yell at a ref or criticize a coach from the stands. But he gave me an earful during every game until I wanted to bounce a soccer ball off his head.

One afternoon, I sat between Mike and Janis, whose daughter was a star soccer player on Matthew's team. The sunscreen on my arms pooled in the creases of my elbows. The dense maple trees on the hillside drooped. On the field, Matthew looked like a zombie.

"C'mon Matthew, atta boy!" Mike yelled. Then he turned to me to give his usual play-by-play. "I can't believe he missed that kick."

"On your left, Matthew. Put some hustle in it!" And to me, "He's sleeping today."

Every time Matthew stepped onto the field, I tensed, prepared for the assault of Mike's commentary. After one of his rants, Janis leaned over to me and whispered.

"I don't think Matthew can help it."

I was stung, not by her comment, but by my embarrassment—for Mike, for myself.

"I know," I whispered back. "He's pissing me off."

Clenching my jaw, I got up and walked to the goal line. I didn't want to listen to Mike anymore. He had been called out as *that* dad who refused to accept that his son was not an athlete.

At home, out of earshot of the kids, I told Mike what Janis said.

"Don't you get it, Mike? Matthew cannot play the way you want him to. You saw him when he ran track. He's slow and weak."

"I wasn't trying—" Mike began, but I cut him off.

"You can complain all you like, but don't complain to me because I'm not listening anymore." I stomped away.

The next day, I called my parents to chat. As usual, I cried and complained about Matthew.

"Karen, please calm down," my mom said. "It's hard to understand you when you're so upset."

While I took a deep breath, my dad offered to mail me samples of his latest miracle vitamins, claiming, "Since I've been taking them, my energy has gone through the roof."

"Thanks, Dad, but I'll pass."

"We're really worried about you," my mom interjected. "Have you been seeing your counselor?"

"Yes, Mom. I have my counselor and we see Matthew's counselor, too."

"If we paid for it," my dad asked, "would you take a few days to go on retreat?"

I squeezed my eyes shut and pinched the skin between my eyebrows. Then I opened my eyes to clarity and strode across the kitchen, phone in hand.

"Mom and Dad. My mental health is not the issue and I won't discuss it with you." I turned and paced the other way. "If you're really worried about me, you'll have to talk to Mike."

I'd never hung up on anyone other than a telemarketer, but

I was too mad to stay on the phone. "We'll have to talk another time. I'm going to hang up now."

"I'm sorry," they mumbled in unison.

"Thank you. I love you both."

I hung up.

At the end of August, I took Matthew and Stephen to my team's annual family picnic held at a colleague's house. Hotdogs on the grill, splashing in the pool, and laughter set the stage for a relaxing day. Sitting on the shaded porch steps, I watched a few adults and a gaggle of kids play basketball in the driveway. Matthew hadn't wanted to join in, but at my urging, he agreed. I wanted to sit peacefully by myself without him clinging to me. And I knew my colleagues would make him feel included and competent. This would be good for him. Isn't that exactly what Mike would say?

Later, the boys ate watermelon on the lawn, and my colleague Tom, the track coach, dropped down next to me. He took a swig from a water bottle and pulled his T-shirt up to wipe his face.

"Karen, um, I made some observations about Matthew that I'd like to share." He stopped to clear his throat. "If you'd like to hear them."

"Sure, Tom. I'm all ears." I turned to face him. I wanted him to know I was prepared for and open to whatever he had to say.

"I know you've been concerned about Matthew. Well, he had a really hard time out there shooting hoops. It was obvious his reactions were delayed." He scratched his beard and ran his hand through his hair before adding, "Significantly." Then with a gentle touch on my shoulder, he said, "I thought you'd want to know."

I looked past him to my sons spitting watermelon seeds at each other. His words should have stung, but they soothed.

"Thanks for your honesty, Tom—it validates what I see all the time." I tried to keep my voice from wavering. "We have some appointments coming up. I think we're going to get some answers soon."

14

Diagnostic Dartboard

Each time the waiting room door opened, a blast of hot air ushered in or out another set of parents and children. Each time, I wondered what brought them to a pediatric neurologist's office, what diagnostic hand they were dealt, how long they had gone without definitive answers. Was it more or less than our three years? I fingered the tweed fabric on my chair. Then I looked down at Matthew's bare legs sticking out of his shorts, surprised he wasn't squirming from his scratchy seat. But he was absorbed in his Game Boy and didn't seem to notice.

I wore a skirt and buttoned blouse to make a good impression. Matthew wore rumpled shorts and scruffy sneakers, although I did make him find a presentable T-shirt. Tomorrow, Matthew would wear his sixth-grade La Salle uniform for the first time.

In the exam room, a petite but solidly built woman in a white lab coat entered and introduced herself as Dr. Lunig. Her highly arched eyebrows gave her face a look of pleasant surprise, and instantly, I felt at ease.

"Mom, what brings you here today?"

My ease vanished behind a cloud of resentment. *I am not your mom.* But I smiled and gave my best performance, explaining my child's litany of troubles. She checked Matthew's pupils and tapped his knees with a rubber hammer. She scrutinized him as he stood on one foot, then the other, then as he walked along a line. She watched Matthew close his eyes and extend his arms, bending them at the elbow to touch his nose. Matthew tackled each task with his usual eager-to-please compliance while I cringed at his every clumsy move. Dr. Lunig's only comments were "hmmm" or "good."

Then we moved to her adjacent office. A floor lamp warmly lit the small space, and a dish of dried lavender on her desk released its pungent sweetness. Matthew collapsed into an overstuffed chair, immediately becoming engrossed in his video game. I sank in the other chair so deeply that I felt like a little kid. Dr. Lunig sat behind her throne. She adjusted her round glasses. A small clock on the wall ticked.

"There is definitely something wrong with your son."

At first, I felt nothing, my senses overrun by her smile, the lavender, the ticking clock, the floodlight of Matthew's video screen.

"I could see it as soon as you came in. It isn't like an eleven-year-old boy not to have an interest in what his mom and a doctor are saying about him."

It hit me: *Thank God. She believes me.* Then it hit from behind: *But what is "definitely wrong?"* Relief and dread fought for control. Until dread went for the jugular.

"It's probably muscular dystrophy, but don't worry, it's not the bad kind—he won't be in a wheelchair."

Her announcement flowed so quickly from her lips that it took me a moment to digest the meat of her message. Images of "Jerry's Kids" flooded my brain.

I realized she was talking again. She wanted blood tests *immediately*, the results faxed to her *that afternoon*.

"Of course. We'll get them done right away." I stood and waited on wobbly legs while she scribbled at her desk. I couldn't look at Matthew, fearing I'd collapse.

"I have a new little puppy," she said, glancing up at me. "He's so cute. You should see him when he sleeps in my arms."

Wait. What?

I nodded, trying to understand the relevance. As she continued, her eyes ping-ponged between me and her notepad.

"My brother—he's a brain surgeon…" She paused, as if to be sure I was impressed. "He accidentally let the puppy out and ran around the yard trying to catch him."

Didn't she just tell me my son might have muscular dystrophy?

"My brother bought him a yellow ball. It's the puppy's favorite toy."

Don't I have to get to the lab?

"My puppy had a little accident on the rug, but I couldn't get mad at him."

Is this a test? To see if Matthew responds to humor?

I dared not challenge her idiocy, as this woman held my child's life—wheelchair or not—in her hands. So my face smiled, and my voice chuckled.

"And my puppy went up the steps all by himself!"

The impulse to scream or bolt pushed me off balance, and

I grabbed the edge of her desk to steady myself. I couldn't believe I was stuck in that room listening to her ramble when my precious son might have muscular dystrophy, and I needed to hug him and call Mike and get blood tests and be alone to cry. Maybe tomorrow the puppy tales would make sense. Maybe I would figure it out later. Maybe the tooth fairy was real.

When we finally stumbled from the office, I wracked my brain trying to find the positive spin. How could I explain muscular dystrophy? What was I supposed to say—"Don't worry, Matthew. You won't need a wheelchair"?

Omigod, will he need leg braces?

Matthew said nothing as we walked to the car and I wondered when he would start needing mobility assistance. We sat with the A/C blasting until the sweat running down his face evaporated. By then, my talking points had gelled, and I turned in my seat to face him.

"Matthew, Dr. Lunig thinks something is wrong with your muscles." I reached over to awkwardly give him a side hug. "But there are medicines and exercises that can help them get stronger. We're finally going to figure this out."

That was my truth. Now that the problem was acknowledged and named, the successful fight against it could begin. Mike, my parents, Matthew's teachers, even Dr. Peterson would join forces. We'd be a team. If Matthew couldn't walk, the team would carry him.

"How do you feel about this, Matthew?"

He shrugged.

"Do you have any questions?"

"Not really."

I drove to my school and told Matthew to go down the hall

to the bathroom, a subterfuge for me to call Mike.

"Mike, it isn't good. Are you sitting?"

For a moment, I thought I'd lost the connection.

"What's going on?" he finally rasped.

"She thinks it's muscular dystrophy." I whispered, unable to amplify the words. Then I quickly explained the appointment and the blood tests, before adding, "I have to go. Matthew's coming."

At the lab, Matthew passed out, and by late morning, I called Dr. Lunig's office to say the bloodwork was done. I waited for a return call to say her suspicions were confirmed, that her referral to a specialist was in the mail. I thought that's how it worked. This was an emergency, wasn't it? But I waited in vain.

The next morning, his first day at LaSalle, Matthew looked dapper in his grey slacks, pin-striped shirt, and polished black shoes, his hair regulation-short and neat. I acted upbeat about his new school but worried about him making friends, worried he'd get teased or become lost.

At work, as soon as the welcome-back bustle subsided, I called Dr. Lunig and left a voicemail. All my incoming calls were routed through the front office, so I checked there for messages throughout the day. I didn't have the nerve to ask the sometimes-testy office staff to page me over the loudspeaker. When I had a moment at my desk, I called Dr. Lunig again, my final message stating I'd be home in an hour. Then I barreled down the highway to make that deadline. At home, no message. I called again and reached a live person who said the doctor was gone for the day.

"But I'm waiting for some test results," I groaned, my nerves too frazzled to hide my exasperation. "She wanted them faxed ASAP!"

"I'll make sure she gets the message."

The next day looked like the first. When I finally got through to a soft-spoken receptionist right before 5 p.m., I was near tears.

"I'm sorry if I seem upset. But Dr. Lunig thinks my son has muscular dystrophy, and I just want to know for sure."

"She does this all the time," the girl whispered.

Closing my eyes, I tried to still the hammering in my heart. I rationalized away my outrage. It wasn't the receptionist's fault. She was very nice. She was trying to help. Knowing the breach of protocol of her comment, in a weak voice, I thanked her effusively and gently returned the phone to its cradle.

That was Friday. The weekend wait was agonizing, and I hovered by the phone. *Shouldn't a doctor call me at home when so much is at stake? Does it matter that it's a weekend?*

On Monday, my waiting and handwringing continued. When I arrived home, I peeked around the corner at the answering machine, afraid to be disappointed again. The red light blinked urgently. I pounced on it and poked "play."

"Hello Mrs. DeBonis, this is Dr. Lunig." Her voice sounded friendly, like she had another puppy story to tell. "The blood tests are negative, so it's not muscular dystrophy. I guess we'll see you back in six months."

The *beeeep* filled my ears. I shook—arms, shoulders, knees. My thoughts raged at the disembodied voice. *You told me my son definitely had something wrong. Your diagnostic skills were so keen, you could tell just by looking at him that he probably had a debilitating, pro-gressive muscular disorder. Then you didn't return my calls for a week. And now I'm supposed to wait six months and do nothing?*

When my shaking slowed, my face cooled, and my mind calmed, a horrible thought slammed me: *If it were bad enough to be muscular dystrophy, but it isn't muscular dystrophy, for God's sake, what the hell is it?*

I called Dr. Peterson first thing the next morning and demanded a new referral. Demanded. Without apology. This time she came through quickly and got us an appointment with a new neurologist the following week.

The next day, we received notice of the date Matthew's special education evaluation was to begin. Mike and I had not yet told him about the testing, so that night, we asked him to sit between us on his bed. I rubbed his knee as we broke the news gently.

"I don't wanna be special ed," Matthew whined, rolling his eyes so furiously, I couldn't tell if it was his tic or his annoyance.

"All it means is that you'll get some help to do your best," I said. "Think how great it would be if you didn't have to spend so much time on homework."

With a side-squeeze, I added, "Wouldn't that be nice?"

I wanted to gag. I hated every wily word that frothed from my mouth. I knew the stigma, knew that kids are cruel to anyone even slightly different, knew that Matthew was an easy target. I didn't want this for him.

More than what I didn't want, though, was what I *wanted*: for him to succeed in whatever setting enabled it. I believed with a few accommodations and a kind, caring academic support person on his side, he could thrive. If straight-A-Matthew was gone forever, I'd embrace his replacement, whatever his grades, whoever he was. I'd work all the harder to convince him of his inherent lovableness.

Matthew flopped back on his bed and pulled the sheet over his head, muffling his voice. "I'm tired of all this testing."

Mike picked up an edge of the sheet and stuck his head underneath. "Matthew, we love you. We want what's best for you."

I wanted to scoop Matthew into a ball like Sonic the Hedgehog. I wanted to wrap him in a towel like I did after his bath when he was little, pressing his shivering body into my warm embrace, pretzeling my legs around him to end his discomfort as soon as possible. I had hated to see him suffer. But Matthew was eleven, and I felt powerless to ease his distress. His problem had grown beyond what a mother's warmth could solve.

A week later, in a new pediatric neurologist's office, a print of a mountain biker mid-air over a rocky path warned: "Love your head? Wear your helmet." In crisp dress slacks and a striped shirt, sleeves rolled up mid-arm, Dr. Steinberg had a fashionable goatee and frameless glasses. After quick introductions, he put his hands on Matthew's shoulders playfully, and then high-fived him with each round of questions about school, friends, favorite TV shows. I suspected his antics were part of his evaluation, and I watched in awe of his mastery. He was also trying to be cool with this pre-teen boy, I surmised, and based on Matthew's laughter, the doctor succeeded.

During the exam, Matthew struggled to complete the simple tasks and he looked drunk trying to walk a straight line. When it was done, Dr. Steinberg picked up a pad of paper.

"Let me show you what I think is going on." He wrote frantically on the pad before holding the paper out to me.

I don't remember much of what he said, but the words spoke for themselves. "Depression" and "paranoia" were scrawled at the top. In the middle, "anxiety/compulsive," which he described as OCD. And at the bottom, circled and underlined multiple times, "Tourette's."

My fears were confirmed, and I blinked repeatedly as the words burned.

"These conditions are comorbid. Do you know what that means?"

I knew, but at that moment I didn't know. I shook my head.

Adding arrows and circles to the page, he explained that the conditions often occurred simultaneously.

"Matthew displays a number of characteristics of each disorder, but he doesn't have enough symptoms of any single disorder to give a definitive diagnosis. I'll send my report to the psychiatrist, and you can discuss next steps with her."

I didn't know whether to laugh or to cry. Either way, a piece was missing. None of the scribbles explained why, ten minutes earlier, Matthew barely could walk a straight line. A nagging voice in my head had a question. But asking too many questions was an inconvenience—especially for a busy child neurologist who had walked to the door to indicate his time was done. Better to end the appointment on a pleasant note than to ask a question about something the doctor had failed to address, wasn't it? If he didn't know the answer, it would be awkward. I would feel bad for him.

I often left unasked questions on the table at meetings, doctor's appointments, discussions with friends about social arrangements. Later, I'd tell Mike or an uninvolved party, "Darn, I forgot to ask something." But it was a lie. I hadn't forgotten. I had chickened out.

This time, however, the nagging voice inside me clawed its way out, and before Dr. Steinberg escaped, the voice pushed through my defenses and burst into the air.

"What about his balance?"

A fleeting, bewildered look flashed across his face. "It goes along with everything else."

That slight hesitation, that blank look, his off-the-cuff answer settled into a dark cloud over my head and followed me around for days. I protected myself with an umbrella of justifications: *Surely, when you're dealing with such complicated symptomatology, not everything will fit neatly into the picture. Surely, some things are bound to be left unexplained.* Still, I appreciated Dr. Steinberg's expert analysis, happy he ordered a brain MRI, "just as a precaution," although it would be weeks before a time slot became available.

That night, Mike's shoulders sagged when I showed him the page of comorbidities. Chattering with nervous energy, I reminded him about the seminar on Tourette's and the *60 Minutes* show on OCD. I wanted so badly to say *I told you so* but being right in this case was nothing to crow about.

Mike and I studied the "physician comments" section of the pink appointment receipt, barely able to decipher "MRI of brain." The rest made no sense: "hyper" something-or-other, and "r/o" followed by a word starting with "l." Only months later did I pull out the pink paper and, with our newfound information, correctly interpret the omens.

Distraught as I was to think of Matthew's heavy load, my confidence in finding a solution increased as our follow-up appointment with the psychiatrist drew near. I expected Dr. Graham to reply to our list of comorbidities with empathic suggestions for treatment and a prescription for a wonder drug, maybe even the magic pill. I envisioned Matthew a few months down the road back to his previous self, my wishful thinking paving the way.

I didn't have Dr. Steinberg's paper with me when Matthew and I sat on Dr. Graham's flowered couch. Did I forget it on the kitchen counter? Did I decide it wasn't necessary? Would it have mattered?

"He didn't say anything to *me* about Tourette Syndrome," Dr. Graham snapped the moment I mentioned the T word. Her eyes flashed behind her oversized glasses.

He said it to me! He wrote it down. He circled it and underlined it!

Conscious of Matthew sitting next to me, I avoided being dramatic as I relayed the gist of the appointment. I felt myself sinking as my former ally poked holes in my liferaft, rejecting my version of the story. With no paper evidence and nothing definitive, it was her word against mine.

The shock of being sunk woke me to a reality: no matter what I said, no matter how convincing my argument, no matter what clothes I wore or how I styled my hair, doctors didn't listen to me *simply because I was a woman*. My years of professional experience and my master's degree didn't matter. The fact that I bore my child and spent almost every day of his life with him was irrelevant. Moms had no clout. In fact, being a concerned mother had worked against me.

I knew doctors would listen to Mike. That our medical practitioners wanted or needed to hear from the father made me sick to my stomach. But I told Mike he had to start coming to all of Matthew's appointments—every single one, no matter how inconvenient. Divide and conquer was no longer a viable strategy. Alone, I had conquered nothing.

Mike readily agreed, and we brought our united front to a counseling appointment the following week. Adam again asked Matthew to wait outside, and when the adults were seated, the atmosphere in the room thickened. Nodding gently, Adam listened as I explained our recent appointments. After I finished, he chose his words carefully.

"I also heard from Dr. Graham. She had some thoughts about what's going on with Matthew."

Adam looked uncharacteristically uncomfortable, leaning forward more than usual, his wide mouth unsmiling. Mike shifted in his chair. I froze.

"It's not a formal diagnosis, mind you. Just a theory she wanted to run by me. I don't agree, but I want you to know."

Steeling myself, I waited.

"Dr. Graham thinks Matthew has schizoid personality disorder."

My first discussion with the psychiatrist flashed through my mind. When she had remarked on the resemblance between Matthew's symptoms and the disorder that sounded to me like schizophrenia, I thought she had used it as a frame of reference.

Like two moms comparing their children's symptoms, but one child has a cold and the other has the flu. When the doctor mentioned a serious mental illness, I had not interpreted that to mean Matthew was mentally ill. I knew that wasn't the problem. And seriously, schizoid personality disorder?

I had been duped. Yet I was partially responsible for this weighty misdiagnosis. In my effort to be agreeable, I had projected agreement. When a doctor said, "mental illness," and I knew it was not, I had an obligation as a mother, as a protector, as Matthew's advocate, to say so. My failure to speak up was a dereliction of duty.

"Let's look this up," Adam said, before Mike or I had time to respond. He pulled the *DSM-IV*-the current edition of the *Diagnostic and Statistical Manual of Mental Disorders*—from a shelf behind his desk, flipped through the pages and read silently, shaking his head. Then he passed the book to us and phrases jumped out at me: "detachment from social relationships... chooses solitary activities... lacks close friends... flattened affect. I could see the similarities. But there was one deal-breaker: "neither desires nor enjoys...being part of a family."

The words eroded the dam that had kept my innermost thoughts in check for the last three years. I had smiled and nodded and thank-you'd and sealed my remarks in brick upon brick stacked at my feet to keep me from bursting. At that moment, the dam collapsed.

"That's ridiculous," I hissed. I straightened my spine. "Matthew does not have this disorder, and we will NOT go back to that doctor again. We need another psychiatrist. NOW."

Adam's mouth was rigid, but his eyes smiled.

Within twenty-four hours, we had an appointment in three

weeks with a new psychiatrist, the earliest Adam could arrange, pulling every string in his network. I found out later how well Adam pulled strings. Only rarely did the highly respected child-psychiatrist and board-certified pediatrician accept new clients. We were lucky to get in at all. If you can call it "lucky."

15

Betrayal

The gray-haired woman in the medical records department picked up a pair of reading glasses from her desk and quickly skimmed the Request for Release of Records I'd given her. She removed her glasses and smiled, one hand fingering a medal on a chain around her neck.

Adam had suggested we request copies of Matthew's files in case any other diagnostic surprises were hidden in the doctor's notes. "Good idea!" I'd said, as if I never thought of it. I *had* thought of it but failed to act because I didn't want to inconvenience the poor person who'd have to dig through the patient files and feed handwritten papers one at a time, hour after monotonous hour, into a photocopy machine. Besides, I assumed Dr. Peterson would know if I made the request. She would think I was mad or dissatisfied with her care. I was. But it would be awkward if she found out.

Adam's directive had helped me swallow my fears.

The receptionist looked up at me, kindness in her eyes. "Is your son having trouble?"

HIPAA was new, confidentiality often breached, and anyway, I didn't care that the clerk asked about Matthew. I needed to talk.

"Yes. A little trouble with schoolwork, mostly," I said.

"I'm sorry. Has it been going on long?"

"A few years."

"That's terrible. Do you know what's wrong?"

My answers grew more complete as her questions got more specific. Eventually, Matthew's whole story spilled out. When I finished, the clerk adjusted a bobby pin in her French twist.

"You know," she said, "I just read an article in *Good Housekeeping.*"

Uh-oh.

"It was about a young boy who was very sick, and his doctors didn't know what was wrong."

Oh no.

Her voice dropped to a whisper. "His symptoms sound similar to your son's."

Please don't!

"It wasn't a disease I'd heard of before. It sounded like leukemia. It was, um ...."

NO!

"Leukodystrophy."

I toyed with a stray paper clip on the counter, avoiding her eyes. Leukodystrophy and Little John had been my secret. What did this mean, for a stranger to share my observation that Matthew's symptoms resembled those of a dying boy?

The woman offered to put a copy of the article in with the other paperwork. I thanked her, hurried to my car, and cried.

A few days later, Lucy, the teacher who confronted me about my possible depression, passed me in the hall on her way to the break room. She pulled me aside and asked if I had ever seen the movie *Lorenzo's Oil*.

I wanted to plug my ears, run from the building, run from my life. I hadn't seen the movie—about a family's discovery of a rare oil to slow the progression of leukodystrophy in their son—but the *Good Housekeeping* article mentioned it.

"I read about it in a magazine," she said. "Do you want me to bring the article in for you?"

"No, that's okay," I said, tears filling my eyes. "I've read it."

Lucy grabbed my hand, her green eyes glowing with concern. I nodded. "Matthew's symptoms are pretty similar."

She pressed her hand to her chest. There was nothing else to say.

A thick envelope stamped CONFIDENTIAL arrived from our HMO a week later. I ripped it open and plopped on the couch, adjusting the pillows behind me. Matthew was changing out of his school uniform upstairs. Stephen played with Legos on the floor behind me. Mike was at work. I slid the photocopies out and reached over to turn on the lamp.

Paper-clipped to the *Good Housekeeping* article was a note with a happy face from the clerk, and I warmed to think of her concern. I labored through Dr. Peterson's almost illegible handwriting, trying to understand the medical abbreviations and jargon. Some entries from earlier that year were perfectly clear:

> *Matthew continues to exhibit fidgetiness and drumming on his thighs, intermittent kicking the exam table, looking all around with eye blinking games. He also exhibits some immature mannerisms and laughter.*

I pressed my lips together. *Eye blinking games? She thinks this is a joke?* In the three years since I first noticed Matthew's tics, Dr. Peterson never once acknowledged something might be off. Just once, she could have said, "You're right. This is suspicious." Just one time and I would have known I wasn't overreacting. But she gave me nothing. Not a crumb.

Coming to another entry, I screwed up my face in confusion.

> *Patient's child psychologist does not feel Mom's concerns are consistent with Munchausen by proxy.*

What?! I mouthed, aware of Stephen on the floor behind me. I sat forward on the edge of the couch, upright.

I'd read about Munchausen syndrome by proxy in my undergrad psychology courses. It's a severe mental illness where a parent, usually the mother, causes or invents sickness in her child to gain attention and sympathy for herself.

I read Dr. Peterson's words over and over, but I didn't understand. "Patient's child psychologist does not feel…" meaning Peterson *did* feel? Meaning she—the doctor we'd trusted since Matthew was born—thought I was mentally ill? That I might intentionally harm Matthew? That she had called Adam to ask his opinion?

"What?!" I sputtered at the paper, hands trembling,

knuckles white. I jumped to my feet.

Stephen popped up from his boy cave. "Mommy, what's wrong?"

"It's okay, honey." I turned around to tousle his hair. "You keep playing. I'm going into the other room to read something."

I stalked to the kitchen, spewing in my mind a stream of invectives. All my years of being the agreeable, uncomplaining parent, all the years I trusted her, and this was her opinion of me? The betrayal was suffocating. And what about Adam? Why didn't he tell us? I quickly checked the dates and saw that their conversation had happened recently, since our last visit. I leaned over the kitchen counter and rested my burning cheek on the cool surface, my heart pounding in my ears.

But did I pick up the phone to complain? Did I march into Dr. Peterson's office first thing the next morning and demand an explanation? Did I tell her she was wrong?

I did not.

Mike sat on the couch that evening when I tried to explain, as I paced and spit and shook. He had never heard of Munchhausen's. He alternately looked up at me and down at the papers in his hand, shaking his head.

"She didn't mean you have it—that munchhouse … thing. She was just…"

"Just what?" I stopped my pacing to stare at him.

"I dunno. Ruling things out?"

"You don't get it." I looked up at the ceiling, hands clenched at my side. Mike stood and tried to hug me, but I shrugged him off.

"You're a great mom, Karen." He grasped my arms. "I know you're mad, but don't let her get to you."

"What if she had accused you of hurting Matthew?" I looked him directly in the face. "How would that feel?

"Karen, she didn't accuse you," he said gently, rubbing my arms.

"Yes. She did."

I broke from his grasp and stormed upstairs.

A few days later, I crept into Matthew's room on a chilly weekday morning to wake him for school. Perched on the side of his bed, I watched his deep, slow breathing. He looked peaceful, not a tic to be seen, and I hated to break the spell. Stroking his buzz cut, I murmured in a sing-song voice, "Matthew, it's time to get up. You slept through your alarm."

His eyes flew open as if he had been awake all along. Pulling his knees up to his chest, curling into a ball, he looked at me.

"Mom, am I going to die?"

I had always tried to be honest with my kids. Honest, with an emphasis on the positive. When they asked, "Will it hurt?" before getting a shot, I told them, "Yes, but not too much and only for a little bit." With every doctor's appointment and every diagnosis for Matthew, I told him the truth in simple but honest terms, cheerleading any sliver of a chance for a good outcome.

But this question.

This question from the sweet lips of a child, *my* child, my Matthew.

With all the doctors and their diagnostic dartboards, I wondered, too, what the future held. Despite Matthew's tuning out during appointments, the gravity of his situation must have seeped in. Even though Mike and I tried to be discreet, Matthew likely overheard the concern and pain in our voices.

His question needed a response, but this time, I chose not to be honest. I didn't know the answer, nor could I fathom that the answer might be "yes." So I chose to help Matthew feel safe just like I did when he or Stephen asked if parents could die, and I assured them. "Daddy and I eat healthy food and wear our seatbelts because we plan to live a long time."

"Matthew, of course you're not going to die! The doctors are going to find out what's wrong and they'll be able to fix it. They'll fix it and you'll get better. Now get ready for school, silly goose."

Back in our bedroom, I told Mike what happened. Without hesitation, he hurried to Matthew's room and wrapped him in a bear hug. I came to the doorway to watch.

"Matthew, I'm your dad and I'm going to protect you. We're not going to let anything happen to you, okay?'

"K, Dad,"

When I got to work, I sat in my ripped vinyl chair, elbows on the blotter, head in my hands. Finally picking up the phone, I called a colleague and prepared her for an intense conversation.

"Matthew asked me this morning if he was going to die."

She waited respectfully while I took a deep breath.

"I didn't know what to say, so I told him no."

Closing my eyes, I imagined the next words, feeling the surrealism of such a moment, of the need to say them, to be forced to squeak them out.

"But what if I'm wrong?"

The question had been niggling at my subconscious for

months, maybe longer, but now it had been aired and could not be retracted, like the smell of sour milk from an opened carton. At the same time, I had to remain detached. Accepting Matthew's death as a possible outcome would consume the strength I needed to finish the fight. I might curl up in a ball under my covers in a dark room, abandoning Matthew when he needed me most.

After taking an audibly deep breath, my colleague replied. "I think you can assure him that he won't die because, right now, that is what you know. As of this moment, Matthew is not going to die."

It was the hope I needed.

When I picked Matthew up after school that day, I revisited the morning's conversation.

"Matthew, remember when you asked me this morning if you were going to die?"

"Yeah."

"Is that something you worry about?"

"No, not really."

"What made you think of it this morning?"

"I don't know."

"Well, it's not something you need to worry about, okay?"

"Okay."

"But if you ever do worry about it, tell me so we can talk."

"K."

I never knew what was going on in Matthew's mind. Even he didn't seem to know much of the time. I hoped he'd feel comfortable talking to me when things got really scary.

And scary was right around the corner at the top of a steep, winding staircase.

I thought it odd at first to have a doctor's office in an attic. Yet I felt at home. Mike and I gave a nod to the restored oak paneling and detailed moldings in the reception area. The stairwell, with its carved handrails, hinted of Murphy's Oil Soap. The attic was spacious and private, and Dr. Handler—Matthew's new psychiatrist—was tall and distinguished, befitting his environment. Otherwise, the appointment was routine—introductions, medical history, finger-to-nose assessments, all while Matthew tapped and fidgeted. His only new symptom was lip licking, a tic that left his lips raw, red, and glistening. Not much came out of that first encounter other than an appointment to return in two days and again the following week. Three visits in seven days. Surely this meant Dr. Handler's attic was to be our redemption.

At the next appointment, Dr. Handler checked Matthew's pupils and dropped a comment as casually as a gum wrapper.

"Well, no brain tumor there."

The possibility never occurred to me.

"His pupils are reacting normally, which rules out the probability of a tumor."

His comment disappeared from my consciousness.

On Saturday, Matthew had a chance encounter with Mrs. Murphy, his former third-grade teacher and friend of my neighbor Janis. Mrs. Murphy—Rhonda—had stopped by Janis' to take their sons on a short hike in the park next door, and Matthew got invited.

A couple of hours later, I heard Matthew clomping up the front steps and hurried to meet him. He kicked off his muddy sneakers on the porch as I opened the door.

"Hey Matthew, how was your adventure?"

"K." He dragged himself in the front door as if he had just run a marathon. He made a beeline for the carpet near the window A/C, and I followed him over.

"Who else went?

"I don't know." He mumbled from the floor where he lay on his stomach.

I could tell he was numb with fatigue. His face was red, streaked with dirt and sweat. His socks, shorts, and the back of his T-shirt were smeared with dirt. I didn't care about the carpet getting dirty—it was an ugly beige anyway. Kneeling on the floor next to him, I found a clean spot on his elbow to rub.

"You're exhausted, aren't you, Matthew?"

He barely nodded his head, and I left him there to rest.

Later that day, I gardened in the front yard while Stephen rode his bike around our small boulevard. Every time he passed me, he waved.

"Hi Mom!"

"Hi Stephen!" I threw him kisses, which he pretended to catch.

Across the street, Janis came from the back of her house, a garden trowel in hand. I called to her.

"Rhonda must have worked them hard today."

Janis smiled and walked over to me.

"I have to tell you what Rhonda told me." She ducked her head and kicked dirt off her sneakers.

"What's that?"

"You may not want to hear it."

"Oh c'mon, now you have to tell me."

"Rhonda said…" Janis paused to swiped away a weed stuck to her shorts. "She said she was horrified at Matthew's deterioration."

I looked at the spent rose blossoms at my feet. My garden clogs were cracked, my knees red and pockmarked from kneeling in the grass. I pulled a loose thread from my cut-off painter's pants. Finally, looking back up at her, I shrugged.

"I'm not surprised. And don't worry, I'm not offended. I'm really glad she told you, and I'm glad you told me. We see the psychiatrist again on Thursday, and I'm going to mention that to him."

The following day, I ran into Rhonda on the soccer field. I thanked her for including Matthew on the excursion and said Janis mentioned her comment. She started to apologize, but I cut her off.

"No, don't be sorry! Your observation was helpful. I hope it'll make Matthew's doctors listen to me."

"I'll tell you what else I observed." Rhonda described at length how Matthew couldn't keep up with the younger boys, that he was awkward, uncoordinated, easily confused. That he seemed "lost."

I nodded at each anecdote. When she finished, she shook her head. "Matthew's a different child than the third grader I knew."

I pictured that child gone forever, and my heart sobbed its farewell.

At our final scheduled appointment with the psychiatrist, when I shared Rhonda's "horrified" comment, Dr. Handler set his clipboard and pen on his lap. He crossed his legs and bounced his foot.

"I think an MRI might be useful. Really more of a precaution—to rule out anything serious."

"We do have a referral in the works," I said. "Our neurologist ordered it."

He picked up his pen. "Why don't I call Dr. Steinberg to speed things up?"

The next day, a hospital representative left us a voicemail. The MRI was scheduled for the following day, a Saturday. Not in three months or three weeks or even three days. One day. On a weekend.

Did that mean this was an emergency?

16

She-Bear

On a jacket-and-sunglasses Saturday morning, we dropped Stephen off with his Uncle Jim, Mike's brother, and headed to the hospital. Mammoth-sized plants filled the wall of windows in the two-story entry, giving off the musky scent of a greenhouse. Most of the seats were filled. I wondered if any of the occupants were having their brains scanned like Matthew.

We found three chairs together. Mike held our jackets and the mug of coffee I brought from home while I checked us in at the counter. When I returned with a clipboard thick with papers, Matthew was curled up in a seat with his Game Boy, his eyes flitting back and forth across the screen. Since the day we made this appointment, I had been glorifying the MRI experience to Matthew, saying it was cool, like a spaceship. I hoped my pretending would work. So far, he seemed unfazed.

"Do you want help with those forms?" Mike asked.

"No, I'm good." I sat down, took a sip of coffee, then placed the cup on the floor and got to work.

When Matthew's name was called, I accompanied him to the bowels of the radiology wing. After I helped him get precisely positioned on the sliding gurney, I kissed his head, gave him words of encouragement, and left.

To this day, I can't figure out why I didn't stay. Were parents not allowed? Could I have stayed if I had asked?

Back in the waiting room, I cautiously reported to Mike that Matthew seemed fine. Sharing a hand squeeze and a hopeful smile, we got comfortable in our chairs and escaped to our own private worlds. Mike read the newspaper. I zoned out on the quiet. The crowd had thinned. Occasionally nurses or other medical people wandered in and out, most wearing white, a few in green scrubs, some in street clothes. They all wore hospital bling—a stethoscope, a name tag, a lanyard. I felt content observing the comings and goings, wondering about people's personal stories.

A thin man in a light blue shirt walked purposefully toward our row of chairs, a lanyard around his neck. What was his job here? Was he coming to sit near us?

"Excuse me, Mr. and Mrs. DeBonis, will you come with me, please?"

For a moment I stared at him, confused. Then his demeanor and tone of voice sank in, instantly putting me on alert. In a shuffle of newspapers, coffee cups, and jackets, Mike and I sprang to our feet and followed Blue Shirt obediently like children summoned to the principal's office. As we fell into step, I gave Mike a look of panic, and he returned a grim expression. Now was not the time for questions. We would do as we were told. We would find out what was going on when we reached our destination, wherever that was.

My pace and stride were calm and fluid, that glance toward Mike the only outward manifestation of my concern. Inside, all that registered was an awareness of my thumping heart. I squelched panicked thoughts from surfacing, reasoning that maybe we just forgot to sign a form. Maybe Matthew freaked out and needed both parents to calm him. Maybe, maybe, maybe.

Blue Shirt directed us into a cramped radiology lab where two stone-faced men in white coats watched us enter. One introduced himself as the radiologist; another sat in a chair before a computer monitor. The rest of us stood. For endless moments, we arranged ourselves. Then, the room held a heart-beat of awkward silence. Then, a gut punch.

"We found a growth."

The words bounced off walls and equipment like hornets caught in a jar, and I froze to avoid their sting. The radiologist pointed to an image of a skull on the computer screen that looked nothing like the pictures in my old anatomy and phys-iology textbooks. *Where is the brain?* The image was an abyss of black, like the middle had been sucked out.

The man sitting at the monitor tapped the screen on another spot, a bright white kidney-bean.

"This is the growth right here."

I tried to make sense of the words, the distorted image, the kidney bean. I couldn't. Shifting my gaze through the plexi-glass window to the adjoining room, I saw Matthew lying inno-cently on the gurney. For the previous half hour, he had lain motionless in the noisy, narrow MRI tunnel. Now, temporarily released from his confinement, he stretched his arms lazily.

I looked back at the computer screen. Scenes from the past three years rolled through my head like a movie reel. It all started to make sense. Perfect sense.

Only seconds, at most, had passed before I realized someone was speaking again.

"It doesn't look malignant and is probably not serious."

Malignant, as in cancer? But not malignant. And not serious... probably?

Should I be happy or sad? Relieved or distraught? Panic buffeted my body from the outside, trying to find a way through my skin. Inside, my opposing emotions canceled each other, leaving a vacuum. I felt nothing.

Mike stood behind me. I wanted to grab his arm, but I stopped myself because, ridiculously, it felt too dramatic. And I knew if the tip of my finger so much as skimmed his shirt sleeve, if I even moved a muscle in his direction, I would collapse. I kept my hands folded, my body still.

The radiologist showed us an image of a healthy brain and compared it to Matthew's MRI. Both were cross-sections, the head split down the middle, front to back.

The healthy brain had prominent intestine-like folds wrapping around what resembled a lamb chop sitting on a bulbous stem. Although I'd forgotten the anatomical names for most of the structures, the image looked familiar.

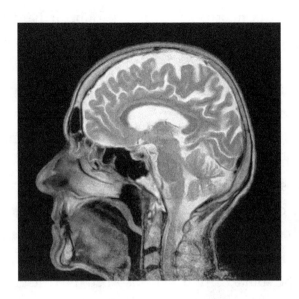

Figure 1. MRI of healthy brain. Image by toubibe from Pixabay

In Matthew's cross-section, I couldn't tell what was what. There were no visible folds, no lamb chop, no stem that I could see. Only the massive black abyss and a thin layer of matter squished into a sliver against his skull.

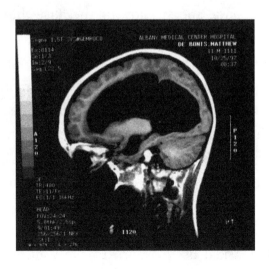

Figure 2. MRI of Matthew's brain

Looking at the misshapen image, I found it hard to believe Matthew functioned at all, hard to believe he was even alive. My observations were ephemeral and abstract, disconnected from emotion, which hadn't yet caught up to reality.

Between the radiology staff explaining more about Matthew's growth and our piecing together information over the days that followed, we came to a rudimentary understanding of the situation:

Inside our brains are four ventricles, cavities that produce and transport cerebrospinal fluid—CSF—through and around the brain. The ventricles also remove this fluid, sending it down through the spinal cord to be reabsorbed into the bloodstream. But the kidney-bean-shaped growth attached to Matthew's brain stem had blocked the exit of fluid. For years, most likely, the CSF had accumulated, blowing the ventricles up like water balloons, a condition called hydrocephalus.

The brain stem, a structure deep within the brain that connects it to the spinal cord, controls essential functions like breathing, sleeping, and swallowing. Because the growth was attached to Matthew's brain stem, surrounded by delicate tissue, it was deemed inoperable. However, it also appeared to be slow-growing and benign, "not serious," as the radiologist said.

One of the white coats said he'd seen the head of neurosurgery at the hospital that morning. We begged to speak with him before we left that day. Then the radiologist asked us for permission to inject dye into Matthew's veins to get clearer images of the growth. "Yes, yes," we both said. "Of course, whatever you need to do."

Blue Shirt asked us to return to the waiting room. As I feared, the moment I broke my inertia, I broke too, fear and grief and regret and love pummeling my body as if I were a punching bag. The instant my foot lifted off the floor, my breath became jagged. High-pitched bleats escaped my firmly closed lips, and I folded in on myself. Seeing what was coming, Mike ushered me quickly into the hallway. "Shhh, Matthew will hear you."

As the door closed softly behind us, I surrendered, heaving with sobs in Mike's arms as he quietly cried. After a few minutes, in a barely audible voice, he said, "You were right, Karen. Thank God you kept looking."

I was right? Omigod, I *was* right. *Dear God, I don't want to be right!*

When my tears subsided, we staggered to an inconspicuous corner of the waiting room and sank into the chairs, clutching each other. In Mike's embrace, my muscles slowly relaxed, my breathing steadied. The paradox washed over me: the horrifying news was redemptive. Matthew had a growth in his brain, but it wasn't serious. Surely there were treatments for it. Surely Matthew would get better. Surely—no, absolutely and definitively—my fight to be heard was over.

Sitting in my chair next to Mike, both of us silent and still, an overwhelming sense of vindication blossomed within me. I felt powerful. Strong. Indomitable.

The power I felt in my core began to grow. Like a mushroom cloud, it quickly surged, flooding my torso and straightening my spine, pulling me upright and erect as if I were a marionette. The boundaries of my body were unable to contain the force, so my legs and arms and head stretched and expanded to gigantic proportions. It wasn't imagined. It was palpable in every cell of my growing body.

I towered—ten feet tall, maybe fifteen. Looking down, I saw

below me the tiny chairs, the puny water fountain, the child-sized restroom doors. I knew what I saw was real because I felt it.

I was *She-Bear*. Those exact words made themselves known to me. I knew that's who I was as clearly as I knew my name was Karen.

Now a massive force, I spread my muscular arms and planted my tree-trunk legs there in the waiting room, eyeing my surroundings menacingly. I roared and snarled at anyone who dared to question my authority. I ripped to shreds those who threatened the safety of my cubs. I challenged potential adversaries to test me and experience my wrath and invincibility.

Then, for a moment, I returned to my body. I was Karen again, slumped in the chair, wondering if Mike sensed what was going on. I glanced sideways at him. He still had his arm around me, his head leaning against mine. He hadn't a clue anything was happening, that his wife was in the midst of a surreal metamorphosis.

She-Bear commandeered my physical body again. From my powerful stance, a handful of minuscule physicians now materialized before me. They trembled and cowered in their ridiculous white coats, stethoscopes dangling about their necks, fearful eyes cast upward toward me. The quaking doctors represented all the wrong diagnoses, the naysayers, the disbelievers. Now, they saw the truth of my power. They understood it was me who saved my son. Hanging their heads in shame, they realized they had let us down. Never again would they doubt me. I, She-Bear, knew my strength.

As quickly as it had started, the transformation ended. I had no idea how long it had lasted. A fraction of a second?

Minutes? Longer? Freaked out, dazed but invigorated, I looked at Mike again, his eyes closed, his breath calm. I said nothing for fear he would think I had lost my mind. Maybe I had—all the more reason to keep whatever weird thing had happened a secret for now.

Finally, on overload from information and images and discomforting words and bizarre experiences, I followed Mike when a nurse summoned us to a hallway to rejoin Matthew. Trying to contain my joy and grief, I hugged him gently while Mike wrapped us both in his arms.

"Matthew, I'm so sorry you had to get that needle in your arm," I said. "I didn't know they were going to do that, or I would have told you."

"That's okay."

"Was the MRI cool like we thought?" Mike asked.

"It was okay."

He was clearly exhausted. With one last group hug, I told Matthew we finally had it all figured out, and we would explain everything in the car.

As we passed through the lobby, a heavyset man in a lab coat stopped us and introduced himself as the Chair of Neurosurgery. He had seen the MRI and explained that Matthew's case was not complicated. Although the growth—called a pilocytic astrocytoma—was inoperable, surgery could alleviate the hydrocephalus, and Matthew would "bounce back." Handing us his card, the surgeon said to call him on Monday.

After "bounce back," I remembered little else. If the doctor hadn't given us his card, I may have forgotten the entire conversation other than those two beautiful words. "Bounce back" became my beacon of light. As frightening as the words *growth*, *inoperable*, and *surgery* were, the strength of Matthew's inevitable bouncing back obscured my fear.

I had read an article in Mike's *Diabetes Forecast* once about a man whose eyes had become so diseased and painful because of his diabetes, he had to have them removed. When he awoke after surgery, he didn't mind being blind because he was ecstatic to be free of pain. This is what I now imagined for Matthew—that the hydrocephalus, although not painful, was so oppressive, its absence would bring relief. I envisioned him waking up after surgery, sitting up and saying, "Phew, I feel so much better!"

We took Matthew out for lunch, not yet ready to return home to our upended lives. In a local diner, country rock playing on the tinny speakers, we slid into a booth with orange vinyl seats. Mike plucked a menu from the wire caddy and gave it to Matthew, saying, "You can order whatever you want."

Mike and I stared at each other across the table. He looked as numb as I felt. Matthew drummed his fingers and gazed into space. I wanted to take his hand in mine but feared it would raise his anxiety about what we had to tell him. So, I playfully tugged down the brim of his Pittsburgh Pirates hat, which he playfully pushed back up.

"Well, Matthew." I forced a smile. "The doctors found a little growth in your brain, which they are going to fix, and you'll be as good as new!" Mike and I took turns explaining a few brief details. Matthew seemed unconcerned until we came to the part about the operation. He sat up straight, his wide eyes rolling.

"Y'mean, I'm gonna have brain surgery? Isn't that dangerous?"

We reassured him the best we could, despite our own fears.

After we picked up Stephen, we let the boys watch a movie on TV so Mike and I could process everything alone in our room. We held each other for a long time. Then, pulling away, Mike held me at arm's length.

"Karen, you know what a growth is, don't you?"

I didn't. I shook my head. He was scaring me.

"It's a tumor. Matthew has a brain tumor."

Omigod. How had I not made that connection? Had the radiologist even said "tumor?" Of course a growth in a brain is a brain tumor. The meaning hit me now with such force, I shut my eyes and sat down on the bed.

I'd feared that diagnosis since I was eight or nine, when the five-year-old daughter of a family friend died of a malignancy that made her eyes bulge like lemons. Then in college, when migraines brought me to my knees to vomit in the toilet, I thought about people with brain tumors. Their pain, I imagined, must be ten times worse than mine. How could they endure the torment?

Thankfully...or perhaps not...Matthew didn't experience headaches or seizures—two typical indicators of brain tumors that might have prompted an earlier MRI. It was another paradox in his unusual case.

Mike and I took turns making phone calls. I had only three people to tell—my parents, Janis, and my work supervisor— and I asked them to spread the word within their respective circles. I had no best girlfriend or bevy of close women to inform.

I'd never had the energy nor made the effort to nurture those types of relationships.

We broke the news gently. "Matthew has a small, benign brain tumor and is expected to bounce back," I said. A part of me wanted to dramatize the telling. *It was a brain tumor all along,* I wanted to scream. *My baby has a brain tumor!* I wanted attention and sympathy, but I couldn't do it. I needed to protect others' feelings. I didn't want to shock the recipients of my calls as I had been shocked, so I tiptoed around the words. Still, it was empowering to state with conviction that we had solved the mystery, and with each call I felt more validated.

17

Why Does No One Cry?

For one glorious Sunday—the day after the MRI—I floated on a cloud of conviction that we'd get our old Matthew back. Our tumultuous past was yesterday's news; the uncertain future was tomorrow's. Today, the only headline I cared about was *Boy Makes Miraculous Recovery*.

On Monday, we set the gears of progress in motion. As much as I wanted to hunker down at home with Matthew to recover from our shock, the four of us went to work and school. Mike and I would miss too many days in the weeks ahead to squander paid time off. We divvied up calls to make, and I canceled my morning classes and groups to stay near the phone. But then I felt trapped. With every trip to the bathroom, I worried about missing a return call. After lunch, I went home.

That night, we compared notes. Mike had first called the chair of neurosurgery we'd met at the hospital. The doctor sounded less concerned about the tumor and more focused on

Matthew's severe hydrocephalus. He explained that, traditionally, this condition was treated by implanting a shunt—a narrow tube—to redirect the cerebrospinal fluid from the flooded ventricle to the abdominal cavity, where the fluid would be absorbed by the body. However, shunts carry risks of infection, bleeding, stroke, and seizures. Therefore, he recommended we investigate Mount Sinai Beth Israel Hospital in Manhattan, which offered an innovative, shunt-free surgery.

The novel surgery—an endoscopic third ventriculostomy (ETV)—sounded simple in theory. A surgeon pokes a hole in the third ventricle for the excess fluid to drip away. Unlike a shunt, no foreign material is left in the body, minimizing the risk of infection. Unless Matthew's tumor grew significantly, which was not expected, chemotherapy and radiation would be unnecessary.

Mike had also spoken to a referral coordinator at our HMO who strongly recommended Children's Hospital in Boston, the only other place in the country to perform ETVs. We were torn by our daunting decision. Both hospitals had sterling reputations, and both were within driving distance, privileges we acknowledged.

We didn't have a computer, so I called Janis to ask about using hers. While our kids watched a movie, Janis showed us how to access the Internet, and we pulled up a picture of Dr. Gordinsky, a pediatric neurosurgeon at Children's Hospital. Her smile lit up the page.

"She's it," I said. I knew she was our savior.

"Before we decide," Mike said, "I want to call the HMO back and grill that coordinator about this recommendation. I want to make sure she's not looking at the bottom line instead of what's best for Matthew." I felt relieved to let Mike take charge. He never shied from asking tough questions, and I knew he'd get his answer.

While we had access to a computer, Mike and I clicked on various websites, trying to understand the medical taxonomy of Matthew's growth. We learned that brain tumors are categorized as either primary (those that originate in the brain, like Matthew's and most pediatric brain tumors) or secondary (those that metastasized to the brain from another part of the body). Half of all primary tumors are gliomas, and the most common gliomas are astrocytomas. Finally, pilocytic astrocytomas like Matthew's, the most common pediatric brain tumor in children, are usually low-grade and slow growing. If Matthew had to have a brain tumor, this was the one to have.

Then a paragraph heading on a page caught my eye, and I pointed to the screen. "Mike, read this." *Benign brain tumors may be deadly when they crowd and damage structures of the brain.*

We went on to read that, while benign tumors in most parts of the body are not especially harmful, because the brain is boxed in by the rigid skull, any abnormal growth can be dangerous, even life-threatening. Since a child's brain is still growing and forming connections, the danger is magnified.

Mike and I grabbed each other's hands. I hoped we had caught Matthew's tumor in time. I hated to think what might have happened if treatment had been delayed much longer.

The next morning, Mike called our HMO and became confident in their recommendation of Children's Hospital in Boston. Picturing Dr. Gordinsky's smiling face, I called her office.

"Hello. My name is Karen DeBonis, and, um, my son was diagnosed with a brain tumor. I'm not sure how to go about this, but, um, we'd like Dr. Gordinsky to do the surgery?"

Our consultation appointment was set for Thursday.

Stephen stayed with his Uncle Jim while Mike and I drove the four hours to Boston with Matthew. In the hospital parking garage, we oohed and aahed over the vibrant animal murals. I asked Matthew to help us remember that we parked on the kangaroo level, although I knew the task was beyond him.

Past the hospital's revolving doors, a giant, glass-enclosed Rube Goldberg-style apparatus dominated the lobby. Colored balls wound their way through a web of devices with *pings, boinks,* and *whirrs*. People scurried about like a mob in a department store. Children of every size, shape, and color, with every imaginable disability, deformity, and disease walked with their parents or rode along in strollers or wheelchairs. All the horrible things that could happen in life were right there, yet everybody went about their business as if nothing were wrong. I didn't see a single tear or sign of distress on an adult face. Nobody was obviously reacting to the drama in which we all were reluctantly cast. What was wrong with them? Didn't they know children were not supposed to suffer like this, and parents should not have to watch?

Mike and I exchanged panicked looks. At the same time, my stomach twisted with awareness that my sick child looked so healthy, that his tumor was benign, that he would soon bounce back. How could I possibly feel sorry for myself or Matthew when these families presumably faced much worse obstacles? I clomped through the lobby wearing their shoes, feeling their pain, reciting a silent prayer of gratitude: *Lord, if this is my cross to bear, thank you.*

When we came face-to-face with the petite, forty-something Dr. Gordinsky, I noted how her computer image had failed to truly capture her dazzling smile. I felt a rush of confidence. I *knew* she was the one to deliver my old Matthew back to me. In fact, all I remember of that meeting was her self-assuredness and the warmth that filled the room. We left with a surgery date of Monday, November 3rd, four days away.

The next day, Friday, was Halloween. I reported to work to tie up loose ends, Groucho Marx glasses and nose in hand. Throughout the day, colleagues approached me with a common refrain: "I can't imagine what it was like to hear your child has a brain tumor." But compared to the dissonance of the previous three years, Matthew's bright prognosis was a symphony. I didn't try to explain. At times, I probably appeared downright buoyant—smiling and basking in the attention—and I worried what people thought of me. Mostly I *was* optimistic and didn't pretend to be otherwise. I thought Matthew might die, and now I expected him to thrive. What mother wouldn't be thrilled?

That night, Matthew trick-or-treated with the neighborhood kids. Surrounded by the usual ghosts and monsters and punk rock cheerleaders, Matthew was his own person, his own creation—an IRS agent. He wore his school uniform, Mike's trench coat, and a borrowed fedora. Like a character in a movie, Matthew knocked on doors and flapped open his coat to reveal his badge that said "IRS. You owe me candy." Then he flashed his smile and people paid him his due. That hallowed eve, my heart burst with a sweet realization: the growth that had nearly destroyed Matthew had not erased his essence.

Over the weekend, Stephen started asking questions about some kind of bug. Typical of six-year-old boys, he was fascinated by disgusting crawly things, and I was used to these conversations.

"Where do they come from? Do they eat?"

I tried to answer, but I wasn't quite sure I followed him. "A slug? Is that what you mean?"

"No, a grub—a white grub."

"They're in the ground, usually. They eat roots, I think."

"No, not that kind of grub," he insisted patiently. "A people grub."

"Honey, I don't know what you mean. What's a people grub?"

"You know, like the grub in Matthew's brain."

"Growth" had translated in Stephen's mind to "grub." When I finished laughing, Stephen and I sat on the couch and talked, a good opportunity to prepare him for the week ahead.

What do you do when you wake up on the day of your child's brain surgery?

You go to the bathroom. Take a shower. Get dressed. Apply concealer under your eyes. Wear a sweatshirt and fat jeans, knowing it will be a long day. Hug your child with gentle fierceness. Pray in a running conversation with God.

How do you feel on the day of your child's brain surgery?

You feel a dictionary full of emotions and sensations: anxious, drained, falsely cheerful, hopeful, numb, spacey, terrified. Hungry, but nauseated. Slightly headachy. Stiff. Tingly. Breathless.

What do you think on the day of your child's brain surgery?

You imagine worst-case scenarios. What if he dies? What if he lives, but he's brain-damaged even more than he is now? Every second holds an ultra-awareness about what lurks ahead. As you dig for clean socks in your suitcase, clasp your watch, pick a piece of lint from your husband's shirt, you are aware. As you caress your son's head that later will be shaved to his scalp, you are aware. As you take one last look around the hotel room before closing the door behind your family, you are aware.

The pre-surgical waiting room boasted a fifty-gallon saltwater fish tank. The baby shark and other exotic creatures served their purpose of distracting us for a few minutes of immersive observation. Then we sat on a couch, Matthew sandwiched between Mike and me.

I picked up a brochure from the end table. Featuring a healthy teenage basketball star, it boasted quick and complete recoveries of children with pilocytic astrocytomas. The star had experienced an unprecedented seizure, which led to an MRI and the discovery of his brain tumor. After his ETV (endoscopic third ventriculostomy—the same procedure Matthew was to have), he was back on the court within a month. *One month.*

I pictured Matthew's handsome face one day gracing a glossy pamphlet, showing him in his La Salle uniform accepting an award for outstanding achievement. In another picture, he'd be crossing the finish line at a track meet, ribbon plastered against his chest, the ends trailing behind him like his competitors.

A bubbly nurse soon approached to apply an anesthetic cream on Matthew's hand and cover it with occlusive tape to make the IV needle insertion less painful. I prayed it worked.

The room filled up. A handsome teenage boy with severely bowed legs hobbled in. Then came another good-looking young man, on half of his face anyway; the other side was swollen like a grapefruit. Other younger boys entered. *What? No girls on Mondays?* Several patients had surgical scars peeking through their hair. *This will be Matthew later today.*

One sorrow after another kept us company. Parents who had lived with my fears. Children who had suffered like my child. Their pain piled upon my own, and my heart sagged under the weight. Then Matthew's name was called.

Here we go.

After Matthew was gowned and in bed, a nurse prepared the IV needle and I squeezed in to hold his free hand. He stared at me, eyes wide with terror. Mike tried to offer a distraction. "Think about scoring a winning goal, Matthew." After the needle was inserted, Matthew said he hadn't felt a thing, and I said a silent *Thank you, Lord.*

Dr. Gordinsky appeared. Mike shook her hand, holding her grip and her eyes a moment too long. "Do your best," he said in a steely voice.

A nurse started the anesthesia, and Mike and I leaned in to kiss Matthew. Another nurse pushed a clipboard of papers toward me. For a split second, two instincts within me fought for priority. One—to sign the papers and appease the nurse, to be the cooperative parent, to keep the wheels of hospital proto-col turning. The other—to be present for Matthew.

"Wait a minute." I put up my hand to keep the nurse and her clipboard at bay. *No one* would come between Matthew and me as he drifted away. I was aware, even at that moment, of the inner pull to be agreeable. With my son on the cusp of brain surgery, I was aware that I had broken my old pattern, that I hadn't said *sure,* that I had chosen Matthew's needs over those of the nurse. "Wait a minute" felt unfamiliar but powerful.

Holding Matthew's hand, I leaned in close and smiled. I wanted my face to fill his visual field, blocking out all the scary things. I wanted my smile to be the last thing he remem-bered, to convey that I loved him, that I was sorry he had to go through this, that I was sorry I hadn't fought for him sooner. I wanted Matthew to know everything was going to be okay and that soon, he'd be smiling back at me.

His eyes closed, and they wheeled him away.

What do you do when your child has been taken away for brain surgery?
You lose every shred of composure you had left.

I had taken the lead with Matthew that morning, tying his gown in back, tucking a blanket around him, fluffing his pillow. Practically bumping Mike out of the way, I'd left my husband no choice but to be my understudy. As Matthew disappeared down the long hallway, however, as I fumbled for tissues in my purse and couldn't pull them out fast enough, Mike took charge. He guided me to the hallway, but by the time we got there, my eyes had squeezed shut. Tears forced their way out with a vengeance onto my sleeves, my chest, my legs. Instinctively, I pulled into myself, hands covering my face, shoulders hunched, feet stuck to the floor. Mike gently eased me forward, his arms protectively holding me. "C'mon, we're gonna get coffee."

In the elevator, I stood in the back, one hand shielding my eyes, trying not to make noise, but loud jagged sucks of air and guttural squeaks escaped. The other occupants probably thought my child had died. In the lobby, people averted their eyes and gave me wide berth, and I wanted to disappear. No one else in the lobby caused such a scene. Other kids were much worse off than my own, yet their parents were stoic. I didn't understand why I wasn't like them.

What's wrong with you people? Don't you know children are suffering in this place?

I tried to freshen my face in the ladies' room but came out crying even harder, so Mike parked me on a bench under a set of stairs and ran into the cafe. Then, coffee in one hand, inconsolable wife in the other, he led us back upstairs.

The surgical waiting area was packed. Coats, coffee cups, and magazines littered laps and end tables and windowsills. Family members talked quietly, read, or stared into space. One family played cards. *Cards? With your child in surgery?*

The only unoccupied seats were smack in the middle of the room, and as Mike led me there, I felt everyone squirming at my distress. Keeping my head down, I repeatedly wiped my eyes and sniffed. Mike sipped his coffee, arm around my shoulder.

After a few awkward minutes, a woman came over and knelt gently in front of me.

"You seem to be having a hard time. May I sit with you?"

She looked to be a little older than me, with brown hair,

black-rimmed glasses, and an angelic smile. I nodded, making room for her next to me. "Thank you," I said, my mouth gummy. Then I laughed, acknowledging the mess I was. The tension in the room broke, and I felt everyone's sighs of relief.

We introduced ourselves and I apologized for making such a scene. The woman dismissed it with a wave of her hand.

"I was that way our first time."

"First time?"

"Yes. My son, Joey, is six and he's getting his fourth open heart surgery."

I grabbed her hand. *How can you go through this over and over?* But before I explained how sorry I was for her troubles, she asked about our visit.

"My eleven-year-old has a brain tumor. He's supposed to bounce back. I feel positive about it, so I don't know why I had such a meltdown."

"It's okay." She patted my hand. "Sometimes you just have to get it out of your system."

We chatted a few minutes before she excused herself to return to her seat, and I profusely thanked her. Feeling grounded, my deep well of tears finally ran dry.

Dr. Gordinsky expected Matthew's surgery to last one or two hours—an unimaginably brief blip of time to fix a damaged brain. The procedure took three hours instead, and when the petite neurosurgeon finally checked in with us to report that the surgery was successful, she explained the delay: so much fluid was present, she'd had difficulty penetrating the ventricle.

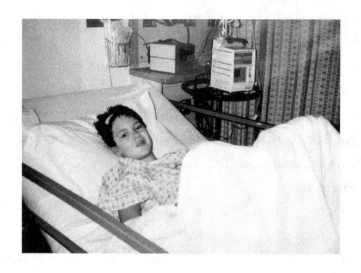

In the recovery room, Matthew was groggy, pale, and puffy, lost in the bed covers—the most beautiful sight I'd ever seen. In his room on the neurology ward, a large arrangement of flowers and get-well balloons greeted us. "Oh, look at this!" I exclaimed, pulling the card from the plastic stick. When I saw they were from Dr. Peterson, I nearly threw them out the window. "She's probably afraid we'll sue her," I whispered to Mike.

After two nights in the hospital and another in the hotel nearby, we drove back to Troy. Eleven years earlier, when we'd brought Matthew home from the hospital as a newborn, I sat in the back of the car to keep his head from falling forward, afraid he would suffocate. A "Baby on Board" sticker hung in the window, and for the entire seven-mile ride, Mike complained other drivers weren't keeping their distance. I felt the same vulnerability on our 175-mile ride back from Boston. I wanted to cocoon Matthew safely at home, to smother him in TLC, to nurture him in a way no one else could.

As soon as I mothered Matthew back to good health, our new lives would begin. I couldn't wait.

18

My Real, Messy Story

Matthew sat on an exam room table in Troy a week after surgery, waiting to get his stitches removed. Mike stood beside him with his hand on Matthew's shoulder, and I leaned back against the table on the other side, forcing my breaths to be deep and measured. I had dreaded this moment since the day I scheduled the appointment. The last person I wanted to face was Dr. Peterson. Being in a room with the person who'd caused me such anguish felt like walking face first into a spider's web. All I could think about was escaping.

Dr. Peterson should have been the jittery one, worried Mike or I would explode or file a complaint or sue. I was in the right and should have felt empowered, but my heart pounded as I picked at a hangnail.

Finally, a rap on the door, and it swung open.

"There he is! What a brave boy you are!"

Smoothing the hair around Matthew's bandage, I returned Dr. Peterson's smile.

Did I detect false cheer in her voice? Did her smile show more teeth than usual? Or was I projecting my fear of conflict onto her?

Mike and I hadn't talked about our expectations for this appointment. Maybe he didn't think there was anything to talk about. He didn't feel betrayed like I did, though. He gave Dr. Peterson the benefit of the doubt that her intentions had been good.

We'd never discussed suing her, either, but I'd spent the days since Matthew's diagnosis imagining the questions I'd answer in a hypothetical courtroom, getting grilled by our doctor's defense lawyer.

> *"Prior to the summer of 1997, Mrs. DeBonis, did you demand that the accused refer your son to a specialist?"*
>
> *"No, I didn't."*
>
> *"Did you ever seek a second opinion from a different pediatrician?"*
>
> *"No," I whisper, hanging my head.*
>
> *"Did you ever emphatically disagree? Did you ever tell her she was wrong? Prior to the summer of 1997, did you ever complain?"*
>
> *"No. No. No."*
>
> *"Let the record show, your honor, that Mrs. DeBonis*

never, in any way, gave an indication she was unhappy
with the care her son received. Move to dismiss this
case."

That courtroom scene never came to pass. Mike and I wouldn't sue; we weren't out for revenge. However, that didn't let Dr. Peterson off the hook. One-on-one, mom-to-mom, I longed to tell her *See, I was right.*

But I dared not let off steam I couldn't control. The times in my life when my anger squeezed its way out of my mouth, my words were accusatory, my tone biting. Most people never saw this side of me, but a handful of individuals in my life might scoff if I were to say I was overly agreeable.

With friends and acquaintances, I more often ghosted them than risk getting snippy. On the rare occasions I subjected family members to my snark, they lashed out en masse and I felt like an outcast. Mike was most often the recipient of my nasty side. I didn't intentionally single him out, but we shared a life together, witnessing the best of ourselves, and, inevitably, the worst. And he was the only one I trusted to still love me, angry warts and all.

I had no practice speaking up to doctors. Once Matthew's medical crisis appeared to be resolved, I couldn't envision telling Dr. Peterson how I felt. Couldn't imagine the words or picture the encounter. Only years later did appropriate statements come to me.

Dr. Peterson, you failed us. I never gave you reason to
suspect I was anything but a devoted mother, yet you
dug your heels in and stopped listening.

How could you dismiss daytime incontinence in an eleven-year-old?

You owe me an apology. More importantly, you owe Matthew an apology.

After our three years of missed- and mis-diagnoses, however, I was unable to speak my mind. My foray into assertiveness—asking for referrals, demanding a new neurologist, standing up to Mike and my parents—turned out to be brief and subdued. My skills had not been honed for the long haul.

When our crisis ended, as I thought it had, so did my need for assertiveness. For the short term, I knew I was safe, guaranteed to be treated with kindness and compassion. No one would have the gall to be unsupportive or demanding of a mother whose child was recently diagnosed with a brain tumor.

And since I no longer had to convince Dr. Peterson that Matthew was sick, I could return to my thank-you-so-much-if-it's-not-too-much-trouble persona. Her negligence—whether it met the legal definition or not—gave me the upper hand. I suspected if I asked for a test, she'd reply, "How soon would you like it?" If I wanted a referral, she'd ask, "Who would you like to see?" If I so much as hinted at being unhappy, she'd tap dance to make me smile. I liked that feeling of power.

Many times over the previous three years, I wished Mike had stepped in and played bad cop to my agreeable cop, that he had demanded Dr. Peterson take my concerns seriously. When one parent is incapable of doing what needs to be done, ideally, the other parent will step in. But we were each stuck in our contradictory perspectives. And we were both accountable for our own actions or lack thereof. Mike's inner reckoning about our journey is "How did I not see?" Mine is, "How did I see and yet not act?"

And what of Dr. Peterson? Where does her blame lie? Physicians in training are taught "When you hear hoof beats, look for horses, not zebras." In other words, assume patients' symptoms are caused by common ailments, not rare ones. Fair enough. I might forgive Dr. Peterson's tunnel vision for two years. But when the animal showed its stripes, as Matthew's did with his increasingly atypical behaviors, her denial of what stood before her was irresponsible, negligent, and life-threatening. I bear no responsibility for Peterson's blindness. That weight is hers alone.

With the passage of time, a gentler, more nuanced picture of how I might have confronted Dr. Peterson came into focus:

> Dr. Peterson, you provided my family with compassionate, effective care from the time Matthew was a baby until his tics and ADHD-like symptoms began. Your initial judgment call not to overreact was a decision many other doctors also might have made. Then you stopped listening. You jumped to a conclusion and got mired in your assumptions. You were, for the most part, a good doctor, a good doctor who made a huge mistake that will impact my family forever.

Even as I imagined the scene, I resisted, compelled to cradle my sense of injustice. But my heart demanded I see beyond my hurt.

When you asked Matthew's psychologist if I might have Munchhausen's syndrome by proxy, perhaps you didn't understand how little my behavior resembled that diagnosis. Perhaps, as Mike assumed, you were covering all your bases, crossing things off your list. Perhaps…

My heart fought me. I could barely think the words.

Perhaps, you were being thorough. Perhaps you truly had Matthew's best interests in mind.

How does one reconcile such extremes of feeling, thinking, and believing?

No one person was to blame for what happened. Not Dr. Peterson, nor Mike, nor me. There are no villains in this story, only flawed human beings making imperfect decisions, being perfectly human.

We kept Matthew with Dr. Peterson until he aged out of our HMO's pediatric care at age fourteen, and we never had reason to complain again.

If any single experience had the power to transform me from Miss Agreeable to Ms. Assertive, my She-Bear encounter would have been it. If my story was a fairy tale, the supernatural visitor would have waved her magic wand so I'd grow thick skin and a strong backbone and live happily ever after.

But mine is a messy-and-real story in which She-Bear appeared when she did me the least good. I needed her on Matthew's first night in my arms and when his tics first appeared. I needed her strength to push the healthcare system for quicker answers, to push Mike to listen, and, more importantly, push me to follow my instinct. But I was on my own during those trying times.

Why did my supernatural transformation happen when it did? The question rattled me for years. Finally, I understood that it validated the supernatural strength it took for me to survive those years; it acknowledged the battle. That fierce mama bear understood it would have been easy for a stronger mother to demand results, but for a mother like me, with such small reserves of courage, the baby steps I took were leaps of great distance.

Like a gazelle.

Part 3

19

New Year, Old Uncertainties

Two months after Matthew's surgery, his horseshoe-shaped scar three inches above his right temple had begun to disappear beneath his hair. That morning, I couldn't see it at all as the four of us slurped our cereal at the kitchen table. Matthew tipped his bowl to finish the milk, and Stephen did the same, followed by an exaggerated "Aah." They both giggled. It was a lull in the frenzy of getting everyone out the door, a familiar routine that made me forget for a moment what the previous year had held.

Matthew stood up from the table and stepped into the pantry. The calm of our morning splintered when, without warning, he threw back his head and wailed, appearing to dredge up emotional pain from deep within his body. At the same time, he slammed the pantry door with such force, it tore a six-foot tall wire shelving unit from its brackets on the inside of the door, sending bottles and jars and cans crashing to the floor.

"Matthew!" Mike and I yelled as we jumped up from the table. Then we immediately softened. Was the brain tumor to blame? We never knew which behaviors were within Matthew's control and which were beyond it.

"You okay, buddy?" Mike asked, rubbing Matthew's back.

"What happened Matthew?" I fought to keep my voice calm. I don't remember his answer, but whatever it was didn't warrant such an explosion of emotion.

The outburst dissipated his anger, so we helped him tiptoe around broken glass and sent him and Stephen to brush their teeth. After they left the room, Mike and I shook our heads at each other.

"What was that?" he mouthed.

I replied with an exaggerated shrug. There was so much we didn't know, so much we'd never know. At that moment, as the January sky turned ice blue, all I knew for sure was that I needed to get on the floor and pick up the pieces of our morning.

Matthew and I had returned to school and work two weeks after his November third surgery. My supervisor encouraged me to stay home through Thanksgiving, but I told her I didn't need more time. I never stopped to think that we had been through a trauma, that I might need time to recover emotionally.

When Matthew had seen Dr. Gordinsky for his one-month follow-up in December, she expressed satisfaction with his surgical outcome. Mike and I peppered her with questions, and she was casual in her recommendations:

Any restrictions? *No.*

Okay to start gym again? *Yes.*

Who should Matthew see for follow-up at home? *Not necessary.*

Tiredness? *Normal.*

Disorganization? *Normal.*

Short term memory? *Will take longer to improve.*

Tics? *Some may be permanent.*

I wondered when the bouncing back would start. Neither Mike nor I had ever had surgery, so we didn't know what to expect other than what we were led to believe. And I believed in miracles. The boy in the hospital brochure had returned to the basketball court a month after surgery. Why wouldn't I expect Matthew's trajectory to be the same?

Dr. Gordinsky wanted to see Matthew monthly for three months, then at six months, at one year, and annually for five years. MRIs were to be done with similar decreasing frequency. Five years was a milestone after which little improvement in symptoms were to be expected. At that point, Matthew should get an MRI and check in with the neurosurgeon every ten years.

At Matthew's February appointment, we told Dr. Gordinsky about the pantry episode and several subsequent incidents I called "rages." She said that type of behavior was common. *Common?* I expected Matthew's symptoms to slowly abate, but so far, they hadn't. I was willing to give it time, but I didn't anticipate expanding the long list of troubles, especially with something unsettling like rages. Having a definitive diagnosis was supposed to make life clearer and parenting easier, but I felt as clueless as ever.

"Pilocytic astrocytoma" supplanted every previous diagnostic hypothesis we'd received. Even ADHD and ADD came off the table after Adam told Mike he closed Matthew's case. The tumor was believed to be solely responsible for every mysterious symptom, and I expected our busy appointment schedule to dwindle.

Matthew's earlier hyperactivity, his sensitivity to touch, and the chewing on his sleeves and necklines remained enigmas. Perhaps the tumor, which may have been growing since birth, was the culprit. Or maybe something else had been going on in his brain—neurons misfiring, faulty wiring. Regardless, and despite the rages, Mike and I believed Matthew's struggles would all soon be behind us.

One afternoon, sorting through a stack of medical papers, I came across the pink appointment receipt on which Dr. Steinberg, the second neurologist, had written "MRI of brain" and several other indecipherable comments. I showed it to a nurse friend who told me the "r/o" meant "rule out." Immediately, the illegible "l" word came into focus. Leukodystrophy. The fatal disease in *Good Housekeeping* that had killed Little John whose progression of symptoms mirrored Matthew's. So Dr. Steinberg had suspected that diagnosis, too. Meaning my instincts had been right.

How blessed we were that Matthew only had a brain tumor.

Later in February, Matthew underwent a neuropsychological evaluation. He scored in the average range for "general intellectual functioning" as well as attention, concentration and, surprisingly, short-term memory. Yet, at home, he forgot to help himself to his favorite mashed potatoes I'd made at his request, although the heaping bowl of carbs sat right in front of him. He forgot to look at the notes I tucked in his pockets. He forgot that he forgot. It was the same tiring story of the previous years: testing and scores did not reflect our reality.

The report identified Matthew's three main problem areas: a low level of arousal (alertness), slow information-processing speed, and fatigue. The recommendations included reducing homework and increasing the time allowed to complete assignments. Unfortunately, the report didn't explain how to parent this chameleon of a child who acted so differently in real life than he appeared on paper.

Given all that Matthew had endured, I should have been grateful for "average." I should have rejoiced that he was able to eat his favorite foods, attend school, play with Sparky. That he could swallow and think and breathe. I *was* grateful. Other children with brain tumors were not so lucky. But it also saddened me to think that Matthew's sharp-as-a-knife brain had lost its edge and we lacked the tools to hone it.

In 1998, my family's vocabulary for thinking about and discussing differences in brain functioning was limited. Ten years earlier, when Matthew was two, Judy Singer, an Australian sociologist with autism, coined the word *neurodiverse*. She intended it not as a diagnostic description, but to recognize the worth of individuals whose brains work atypically. A decade later, American author Harvey Blume popularized the term in *The Atlantic* and wrote, "Who can say what form of wiring will prove best at any given moment?"

I'd never heard of *neurodiverse* or *neuroatypical* when our family might have benefitted from the understanding. I didn't know about *ableism*, a term coined by feminists in the 1980s. Lacking familiarity with computers and the Internet, we didn't know how much we didn't know. We picked up brochures from doctor's offices, read materials handed to us, talked to friends and colleagues who had expertise we lacked. The river running beneath the information we received was our understanding that Matthew's regression was not permanent.

If Matthew had broken a leg when he was still a gazelle, and we were told he'd heal, I'd expect him to run again. If, as a straight-A student, he suffered a concussion, I'd expect his grades to wobble, then rally. Mike and I accepted Matthew where he was in his brain tumor recovery, but we anticipated someday he'd be running track and acing his classes again.

Either way, Matthew was "cooperative, polite, and articulate," according to the report. I valued those characteristics more than intellectual functioning, and I was comforted knowing the best of him was intact. Mike and I wouldn't love Matthew any less if he never progressed further than where he was. But we didn't expect that to happen. We believed he was going recover completely. In the meantime, I searched for belonging.

In the grocery store of all places, I picked up a brochure for a local support project for children with brain injuries. I learned that a Traumatic Brain Injury (TBI) is caused by an external force like a blow to the head, while the damage caused by a disease or tumor is an Acquired Brain Injury (ABI, though these are often grouped under TBIs). I called and spoke to the director. She rambled enthusiastically about her collaboration with multiple school districts, about IEPs (Individualized Education Plans) and special education programs, about coordinating services with PT, OT, and speech. After a few tries, I finally interrupted her spiel.

"It sounds like a wonderful program, but not what my son needs. His doctors expect him to bounce back. He really just needs to spend time with peers who understand what he's going through." What I didn't explain was that *I* needed peers—other parents who understood what *I* was going through, who understood how it felt to be me.

"I don't mean to be rude," she said, "but a doctor cuts into your son's brain and they tell you everything will be fine?"

Immediately, I felt foolish for believing our neurosurgeon, ashamed for not being a more astute mother.

"You'd better come right in," she continued when I didn't answer. "I'm free Thursday at four."

Two weeks later, on a dreary March afternoon, Matthew and I walked past rows of empty yellow buses in the parking lot of a brick school building. We stepped into the dimly lit front hallway, our footsteps echoing on the smooth floors. Bulletin boards at every turn held thumbtacked announcements. A hand-drawn sign, "Brain injury support group" pointed us down the left wing.

Just as we found the correct classroom, an energetic, red-haired young woman appeared at the door, a group of youngsters trailing behind her.

"Hi, I'm the art therapist," she said, raising her right hand full of paint brushes. "We're on our way to the art room." After quick introductions, she swept her arm grandly toward Matthew, inviting him to follow her, and he happily fell in line.

As I entered the classroom, a woman with salt-and-pepper hair wearing an oversized flannel shirt motioned to me from a circle of seated adults. I shook off my coat and eased into a chair. One by one, parents introduced themselves and told their children's stories—a car crash, shaken-baby syndrome, encephalitis, a head-first fall from a grocery cart. I stepped into the shoes of each parent as they talked and felt like I had walked a thousand miles. Awaiting my turn, I fiddled with my rings. What could I possibly say? That Matthew was doing great? That he had no restrictions? That he attended a tough private school? It wasn't fair that Matthew was doing so well, yet we were there precisely because he was *not* doing well.

Finally, when the group turned to me, I shared the basic facts of Matthew's situation, trying not to paint a picture too rosy or too bleak.

When the children returned to the room, I noticed all of them had limps or crooked smiles or scars—evidence of their injuries. Then there was Matthew, in his rumpled but respectable khakis, pin-striped shirt, black dress shoes. I wondered if he felt as out of place as I did.

Where was my tribe of parents who counted their blessings and came up just a little short? Where was Matthew's cohort of highly functional kids who had lost a little ground? I didn't think the brain injury support group met either description, but it was all we had, so we stuck it out, Mike and I taking turns bringing Matthew.

In May, I settled into a chair in the adult circle. A new participant talked about her three-year-old son who had been in a coma following a near-drowning in the family's pool.

"He recognized me this morning! And he knew his name!"

I didn't know how to position my mouth, what to do with my eyebrows, where to put my hands. Should I smile because she smiled? Because all the other parents smiled? Did my face reveal my horror at what she had lost? Tears stung my eyes, and I knew I couldn't hold them back for long. Slipping out a side door, I found myself in the dark cafeteria kitchen. I huddled next to the gleaming ovens, shaking, arms hugging my middle.

A young woman poked her head in.

"Are you okay?"

I shook my head and she stepped into the room.

"Are you a counselor?" I whispered.

She nodded as she stuck out a hand and introduced herself, but I couldn't acknowledge her gesture. Sobs forced their way from my throat, and I doubled over before sinking to the floor. She sank with me, rubbing my back, not saying a thing. "It's too sad," I choked out. "These families have suffered so much. My son is so healthy compared to their children."

She acknowledged my right to feel grief and sadness regardless of others' losses. I knew that was true. But my capacity to absorb pain was maxed out. The other parents' traumas wouldn't allow me to heal from my own.

We left that night and never went back.

Continuing the quest to find our place in the world of brain injury, I read about intensive brain retraining programs, also called cognitive rehabilitation. The closest site I found was in New York City, a three-hour drive south. Patients met twice weekly in two-hour blocks for six to nine months. For Matthew to participate, he'd have to drop out of La Salle, and I'd need to quit my job. Our family couldn't afford that financial hit and I couldn't tolerate the emotional split.

Some moms travel the globe in search of treatment or a cure for their sick child. I'd read their stories. I saw them at Children's Hospital. One such mother in a black burka wore a beautiful gold filigree face-covering unlike anything I'd seen even in magazines. She crouched behind a man gesticulating to a translator. The mustachioed father gently swung a baby carrier stuffed with pink blankets and an infant with a swollen head.

I was not that mom. I wasn't a world traveler, and my sense of direction was so bad, I didn't trust myself to navigate a big city. What good would I be to Matthew if we both got lost? Plus, I wouldn't intentionally abandon Stephen to move away with his older brother, even temporarily. Maybe if Matthew needed to relearn how to speak and walk and eat, I'd have hopped on the nearest bus to Timbuktu. But he didn't, so I wouldn't. We had to make this work on our own turf.

20

Deflated Hopes

Almost a year after our rude introduction to the world of brain tumors, I relaxed in the living room one evening watching a taped *Oprah* show. The volume was set at a whisper so it wouldn't distract Matthew. Ostensibly, he was doing his seventh-grade homework upstairs. Given the amount of tapping I heard, however, I doubted he was being productive.

With academic accommodations and two supportive sixth-grade homeroom teachers, Matthew had limped through his first year of middle school with passing grades. In seventh grade, the workload was heavier, the expectations higher. Changing classrooms for each subject meant Matthew faced a different teacher, personality, and teaching style multiple times a day. The demands weighed heavily on his shoulders, more than we realized.

Stephen had finished his second-grade homework before dinner, as usual, and was upstairs showering under Mike's supervision. I planned to check in on Matthew at the next commercial break. Until then, my feet tucked under me on the blue loveseat, I reveled in the rare solitude.

I heard a creak and turned toward the stairs. Matthew was tiptoeing down, still in his school clothes, his black socks collecting white Sparky fur from the carpet. When he saw me looking at him, he paused.

"Mom, can I tell you something?"

"Sure, Matthew."

I patted the cushions next to me and turned off the TV. The room became noticeably darker. Avoiding eye contact, Matthew sat down stiffly, fumbled with his fingers and did a few wrist rolls. Despite his surgery, most of his tics persisted. I shifted sideways to face him, then waited, giving him time and space to share what he wanted.

He took a shallow breath and spoke quietly but clearly.

"Today, I tried to kill myself."

The world stopped.

A million scenarios of what Matthew meant by "tried" flashed through my mind, but none of them ended with this child before me, visibly unharmed, whole and clean and calm.

"Oh honey." Taking his hand in mine, I stroked his fingers with my thumb. He sank back into the loveseat, fat tears rolling down his face. My own tears clouded my vision before spilling over. I waited, afraid to hear more, knowing I had to.

"I got so frustrated with my life and with homework." He banged his head against the back of the loveseat, and his free hand flopped onto his thigh. "I ran around the house from room to room looking for something to hurt myself with."

I imagined his wild look, his frantic desperation. An iceberg of anguish lay below the surface of my sorrow. What behemoth lay beneath Matthew's surface, that he would want to end his life?

"Honey, where was I? Was this before I got home from work?"

"Yeah."

That afternoon, I had attended a faculty meeting, and Matthew took the bus and beat me home. When I got to our house after picking up Stephen, I checked in with Matthew. He looked perfectly fine. There was no indication anything was awry, so I rushed around as usual to start dinner, monitor homework, gather a load of laundry.

"I was looking for something sharp," Matthew said in a monotone. "So, I took one of your seam rippers."

Oh my god.

My sewing machine table was in Matthew's room. To keep him company while he did homework, I often sat on his bed mending clothes, including ripping out stitches. He had seen me use the seam ripper.

I pictured him holding the blue handle, contemplating the sharp point and its consequences, just as I had done not that long ago with my pink razor blade.

I waited, breathless, for him to continue. For a moment, we were suspended in time.

"I wanted to cut my jugular vein."

My poor baby!

"But I put the seam ripper back. I didn't know where the jugular was."

God help me, but I wanted to laugh. Thank God they didn't teach the location of the jugular vein in health or science class, or if it had been taught, thank God for Matthew's faulty memory.

"Matthew, I am so sorry you felt that way." I put a throw pillow on my lap. "Here, put your head down."

He curled up sideways. I stroked his hair and his face while tears continued to flow for both of us. *What if he had done it?* I had to squeeze my eyes shut against the thought. I ached for his aloneness, knowing intimately the awfulness of it. The thought of him running from room to room in such anguish, alone, made me the saddest I've ever felt.

"We'll change things, Matthew. Homework doesn't matter. I don't care if you never do it again. The absolute most important thing is that we help you feel happy again."

"Okay," he mumbled, his body relaxing into mine.

We stayed in those positions for a while. I wished it could have been forever.

"Tell you what, Matthew, no more homework tonight. How about if you veg in front of the TV until bedtime. I'm going to say goodnight to Stephen and talk to Dad. I think it's important that Dad know about what happened. Is that okay with you?"

"Yeah."

I kept my hand on his shoulder, afraid to leave.

"I'm going to go upstairs and do that, then I'll be right back down. Okay?"

"K, Mom." He lifted his body to let me stand.

I hesitated. Should he be left alone right now? Even for a few minutes? From my mental health training, I knew a certain question needed to be asked directly. Without subterfuge.

"Matthew, you'll be okay if I leave you for a second, right? You won't do anything to hurt yourself, will you?"

222

"No, Mom," he said in a voice that suggested I might be overreacting. But I knew the stakes were high, and I knew I had to err on the side of caution.

I handed him the remote and walked heavily upstairs. When I told Mike, he turned white. Then he stormed into Matthew's room, rummaged through my sewing table and returned to our room with my seam ripper, sewing scissors, and pin cushion. He buried them in his dresser drawer. I knew he wasn't angry at Matthew; I suspected he was as furious at his own power-lessness as I was at mine.

After kissing Stephen goodnight, Mike and I went down-stairs together. Mike sat next to Matthew, enfolding him in a hug.

"Mom told me about what happened." He pulled back to look Matthew in the face. "We don't ever want you to do anything to hurt yourself." His voice wobbled. "We love you, Matthew, don't ever forget that, okay?"

I turned off the TV, then squeezed in with them.

"We'll definitely lighten up," Mike continued.

"Yeah, Matthew," I added. "No more homework until we come up with a better plan."

We scrunched together for a few minutes. I assumed Mike, like me, reeled from the aborted disaster. Matthew was proba-bly absorbed in the interrupted TV show. For him, I believed, the crisis was over. He had told us the important information, and he knew we would take care of it. *Please*, I imagined him thinking, *let me get back to TV where my real life doesn't exist.*

The next morning, Matthew got up and dressed for school as if nothing had happened. What is the protocol after a night like ours, other than not leaving a child alone? I wasn't sure, but a return to routine seemed appropriate, especially since Matthew had said he was fine and my instinct told me that, at the moment, he was.

Adolescent mental health guidelines recommend a school be notified when a student has an intentional brush with death. Mike and I discussed what to say. I explained the definitions of suicide-related behaviors as I understood them: An "attempt" meant actual harm had been done. "Ideation" was a thought or plan without action. "Gesture" lay in-between—Matthew holding his blue-handled weapon, intending to use it, but not following through.

"Matthew made a suicidal gesture last night," I told Brother Chris, the bearded and bespectacled middle school principal, our biggest advocate at La Salle. He asked for permission to tell the school nurse, who called me within minutes.

"Sometimes, when this happens," the nurse said gently, "we develop a support plan to ensure the safety of the student." It was a stark reminder of the seriousness of the situation.

"Thank you, but I don't think that will be necessary." Matthew was too eager to fit in at school to do anything that might make him stand out. If he attempted to harm himself again, it would happen at home. "We have a counselor I'm going to call. But I'm glad you know, and, of course, call Mike or me immediately if anything...happens."

When I got to work, I called Adam for a crisis appointment and cleared my afterschool schedule for the next several weeks. Mike and I monitored Matthew's homework and stress level more closely, writing daily excuses for unfinished work. Matthew still fought us over the excuses. He *wanted* to do the work. He *wanted* to be like the other boys. But Mike and I knew we had more to consider than simply an adolescent's need to conform.

As seventh grade wore on, we accepted another reality: Matthew still needed special education services. We had halted the progress on our earlier application as soon as Matthew received his diagnosis and sunny prognosis. We had naively believed he would no longer need extra academic help. So we submitted a new application, and, as it turned out, we were right, in a way. When Matthew reluctantly submitted to the testing, the results did not qualify him. He scored too high.

Then I learned about 504 plans, shorthand for Section 504 of the Rehabilitation Act of 1973. This federal law requires school districts to provide accommodations and services to students with any disability that interferes with their capacity to learn in a regular classroom. Private schools must comply with the law if they receive federal funding, as La Salle did. Our application was approved too late to implement a plan that year, but I breathed a little more deeply over the summer, knowing support was in place for eighth grade.

In the meantime, life was a series of adventures. One day, I arrived at La Salle to pick Matthew up after school as we had discussed at length that morning. Each morning I wrote two copies of a note reminding Matthew of the transportation plans for the afternoon. The note might say, "Mom pickup 3:15," or "Bus today." One note went in his shirt pocket and an identical sticky note went on his binder, which he was supposed to re-stick in his locker when he got to school. Before Matthew left the house with Mike, I gave him several verbal reminders, and when Mike dropped him off, he gave a reminder, too. But when I pulled up to school later in the day, I never knew what to expect.

Matthew liked taking the bus, and life would have been easier if he took it all the time. When he had a counseling appointment or had to stay after school, however, we were forced to make alternative arrangements.

One such day, the sticky note said, "Mom pickup 4 p.m." When I arrived, Matthew was nowhere to be found, even after Brother Chris unlocked the main office and paged him. I drove home in a panic. Did Matthew have his key? Did he know what to do if he got locked out? He had a two-block walk from the bus stop on a main street to our house. *What if something happened?*

When I got home, Matthew wasn't there, so I called Mike at work.

"Mike, Matthew's lost again.

"He probably took the bus."

"But he should have been home by now."

At my urging, Mike left work and drove to La Salle. In the meantime, I wondered if I should head out and cruise the streets. But what if Matthew called? What if Mike called? And what if Matthew got home and I wasn't there, and he was unable get in? Plus, I had to pick up Stephen from his after-school program before they closed.

Then I looked out the front door and saw Matthew moseying up the street. I wanted to race out and throttle him, but by the time he got to the front door, I felt more rational.

"Hi Matthew! I was worried. Did you forget that I was going to pick you up today?"

"Today?"

"Yup. Remember, I wrote you two notes. Is it in your pocket?" (I could see it sticking out.)

"No, I don't think so."

"Yup, there it is. Read it."

"Oh."

"What about the sticky note for your locker?"

"I don't know."

"Let's see if it's still in your binder." (It was.)

"Matthew, didn't you see this?"

"I guess not."

I reminded him that every day after class, he was to look in his pocket for a note and take a moment to think: Will Mom be picking me up today?

Then, with urgent instructions to answer the phone if it rang, in case it was his father, I rushed out the door to get Stephen.

These transportation debacles went on for most of the year until Mike and I got beepers. We had a code system: 311 meant to call the other person before the end of the day; 511 meant to call as soon as possible; 911 indicated a real emergency. A couple of times, I got a 911 from Mike on my beeper when I was driving. My heart in my throat, I rushed to find the nearest pay phone, thinking Matthew had suffered an accident or a seizure, or that an equally dreadful thing had happened to Stephen.

As it turned out, Mike only wanted to check on the evening pick-up schedule. The man is lucky to be alive.

Finally, our investment in cell phones saved my sanity.

Nine months post-surgery, Dr. Gordinsky cleared Matthew to play sports again, much to my chagrin. On the soccer field, Matthew moved in slo-mo, unable to keep up with the action. Heading to our car after one game, we passed another father who announced to everyone within earshot that "the kid in the blue shorts" screwed up every play, shouldn't be playing, lost the game, etc.

Mike stomped up to the man, taller than him by a head. "The kid in the blue shorts has a fucking brain tumor. So get off his case, goddammit." The other father looked stunned. The parents around him looked away or at the ground. This was language Mike seldom used, especially in public, and I felt infinitely proud.

In November, I pleaded with Mike for Matthew to sit out the hockey season, but I was outnumbered. Gordinsky approved it, father and son wanted it, so I let the puck stop there. After that season, Matthew lost interest in playing organized sports, and I finally cheered with enthusiasm.

The constant demands at home competed with the immense needs of the students at my school. My schedule of classroom lessons and support groups was manageable and enjoyable, but the crises overwhelmed me. The second grader who assaulted students in her classroom and needed to be restrained. The fifth grader who came to me in tears because she hated her life and had tried to choke herself in the bathroom next to my office. The three brothers who got off the morning bus and ran to my office to tell me, "We had child abuse last night by our mom, and our dad said to tell you."

I slept poorly, again plagued by vivid dreams that left me exhausted when I awoke. Driving to work was dangerous many mornings. Fighting to stay awake, I blasted the radio, opened the windows, let the cold air bite into my cheeks. At work, desperate for energy, I made frequent trips to the coffee machine and often the vending machine. Then my day ended, and I fought sleep on the way home from work, too, dreading the long, tiring evening ahead.

Matthew played drums in the La Salle band, an extracurricular graded class that took place before school most days. Mike and I worried the commitment would overload him, but were happy he had a place to shine. To build his skills, Matthew also took private drum lessons.

One night, I served dinner early, as usual, to get Matthew to his lesson. He kept wandering away from the table, and I kept calling him back. When he sat down, I had to remind him several times to eat. After he finished, I told him to get his drumsticks and book, and I went out to start the car.

Sitting in the car in the driveway, I watched as Matthew walked out the door empty-handed and pulled the door shut behind him. I rolled down the window and yelled up to him.

"Matthew, where's your stuff?

He looked at his hands and trotted back to the house. I watched him jiggle the doorknob, dig in his pockets, and turn to me with a shrug, the action unfolding like a silent slapstick film.

"Come here and get my spare key," I called.

He hurried down, hurried back up and disappeared in the house for a moment. When he came out, he left the door wide open.

"Matthew, shut the door. And make sure it's locked!"

We finally got on our way, fifteen minutes late. I gripped the steering wheel, gritted my teeth, and reminded myself: *He has a brain tumor. He has a brain tumor. He has a brain tumor.*

In the fall of eighth grade, Matthew was accepted into the highly regarded La Salle jazz band. A week before Christmas, the band played in the mall, and Matthew had a drum solo.

I stood with Mike and Stephen among the spectators near the food court.

"There's Matthew," I said, pointing him out to Stephen, eight. "Do you see him?"

"Yeah," he said, air-drumming.

The mall bustled with holiday shoppers, their heavy winter coats slung over their arms, hands laden with red and green department store bags. The band played tunes like *Funky St. Nick* and a jazzed-up version of *God Rest Ye Merry Gentlemen.* Occasionally, Matthew's head peeked out from the back where the percussionists took turns on the maracas and triangle. Finally, the horn section kicked off the melody of Matthew's song. When all the instruments stopped and his singular drumming filled the mall, I didn't even try to hide my emotion. Mike put his hand on my shoulder and whispered, "That's our boy." "Our boy" smiled and beamed and grimaced, his tongue wiping his lips in concentration, his expert hands a blur.

Matthew earned straight A's in both bands. This counted toward his overall average, bumping up his GPA. Through his 504 plan, he also had the support of a consultant teacher who worked with Matthew after school several days per week. The boost in his average was enough to admit him to the eighth-grade Junior Honor Society. It came as a sweet surprise, given the papers he still brought home with Cs, Ds, and a rare F circled in red. It didn't add up for me. I couldn't reconcile his struggles—despite the extra support—with membership in an academic organization. I wondered if someone in authority at La Salle had pulled strings or if teachers fudged grades. I didn't care, and I wouldn't question. Matthew deserved the recognition. He fought more to get through each day than many adults fight in a lifetime.

At the Honor Society ceremony, Mike and I strained to see Matthew sitting with his class in the crowded gymnasium. When his name was called, he stumbled to the front of the room and looked straight ahead, barely suppressing a grin. Other students waved at their parents or smiled at their friends, but Matthew played it cool. Scenes from our recent years flashed through my mind—my frustration with and hopelessness about Matthew, my anger at him. And yet there he stood, practically glowing.

21

At Odds with Motherhood

I sat on the floor of my parents' living room, surrounded by my extended family, all of us stuffed from my dad's grilled salmon and my mom's layered potato casserole. Mike sat near me on the couch. Two years post-surgery, Matthew watched TV with Stephen and their cousins in the basement. The upstairs conversation, dominated by my father and brothers, ran the typical gamut from world peace to the theory of relativity. I can almost hear my dad pontificating on his "Ten-to-the-28th Atoms" theory about the intricacies of the human body, and I can see my mom's exasperated look. That's when she interjected a "Myers-Briggs" comment, and I started to pay attention.

Mom was infatuated with the Myers-Briggs personality inventory, a forced-choice questionnaire to help individuals understand how they perceive and interact with the world and with others. She had been introduced to the assessment tool at a religious program, then took the training to become certified to administer it.

"Your father is an INTP (Introvert/iNtuitive/Thinking/Perceiving), so he feels useful when he shares information. I'm an ESFJ (Extrovert/Sensing/Feeling/Judging), and I understand better what I'm thinking by talking with others."

"Mom, can you give us all that test now?" I asked, sitting upright. "Can you do it in a large group like this?"

She happily complied.

When I finished answering the questions, I scored my results and looked dubiously at the four-letter acronym they suggested. I didn't try to understand the last three letters where my scores were somewhat ambiguous. But the first letter—"I"—bowled me over. *Introvert? Me?* I loved throwing a good party. I loved public speaking. How could I be an introvert? I tried to recall learning about personality types in college but drew a blank. How could I have a four-year degree in psychology and not know this about myself?

I had spent so many years being what I thought others expected me to be, I had no idea who I really was.

"Mom, you won't believe this. I'm an introvert."

"I would have guessed that, Karen." Her smile reminded me how often she knew me better than I knew myself.

As Mom read a list of introvert characteristics from her materials, bits and pieces jumped out at me: "prefers doing things alone...takes time to reflect before acting...active inner world...seen as reflective or reserved."

I listened intently. Parts of the description rang true, but other parts didn't fit. My mom must have noticed the confusion on my face.

"The easiest way to think of it, Karen, is knowing what gives you energy and what depletes your energy." For a moment, she shuffled her papers. "After a party, do you feel energized or depleted?"

"Exhausted."

"After time by yourself, do you feel energized or depleted?"

I thought about a recent day when the kids attended summer camp, Mike was at work, and I had the day off. I spent eight hours weeding a pachysandra bed in the side yard. No music, no conversation, no interruptions. Only short breaks to eat, drink, and use the bathroom. It was one of the most enjoyable days I'd had in years.

Gripped by a sudden sadness, I said, "I love being alone."

No wonder motherhood was harder than I imagined. Matthew's endless nights of screaming as a newborn, his wildness as a four-year-old, the years of constant worrying and cajoling and cheerleading. With no down time, I had no time to think, no time to be, barely enough time to do what needed to be done. I thought of the afternoons when I was desperate for a nap but felt too guilty to take one, so I binged instead.

I doubted anyone considered motherhood easy. Like me, most of the moms I knew complained about bake sales and fundraisers and not having "me time." But they rarely said "no." They laughed off the demands, apparently enjoying their role in the circus ring. I loved my kids, but I wished we lived on a desert island where we could enjoy each other's company without ever having to sell a raffle ticket or expensive rolls of wrapping paper.

When I expressed my frustration and exhaustion to my mom over the years, she urged me to get away, to go on a retreat. I needed a break for certain, but she always suggested religious or spiritual retreats, which had no appeal to me. I never explored other options because getting away didn't seem feasible anyway. I didn't want to dump my weekend childcare or household responsibilities on Mike. If I disappeared for a few days, my absence would prolong the disruption and chaos of our current house projects. I longed for the finished products—the rebuilt front porch steps, the repaired ceiling plaster, the basement storage closet—and I wanted to actively support us in reaching those goals.

When I complained to Mike about the tasks facing us on a weekend, he'd say, "I can do this without you. Go have fun." But then what? I sit in a lounge chair in the yard while he crawls on his back in the broiling attic to run wire? I sip chardonnay with friends while he puts down his paintbrush and fixes lunch for the kids? What kind of partner does that? I signed the deed on our old house, too, and I had responsibilities to fulfill. Abandoning him for a weekend get-away was not a choice I was willing to consider.

I did travel for a few days annually to attend a professional health education conference. Energized by like-minded educators, by lesson ideas, by drinks in the bar, by a long soak in a clean tub, I usually returned home refreshed and revived. But one year when the kids were younger, I got home after a long drive to find Mike mopping up the bathroom where the toilet had overflowed *again*. Watching from the hallway where it was dry, the kids wildly running around behind me, disgust bubbled up within me. At that moment, I wanted out. I wanted to jump back in the car and drive away.

When my mom suggested I go on retreat, I didn't tell her—because I hadn't admitted it to myself—that once I tasted freedom, I might never come back. A structured, professional conference was one thing, but what if I soul-searched and found my spirit yearning for something else? What if the "something" didn't involve an old house, a husband, and two children? What if I wasn't cut out for motherhood? Buried in my subconscious, I knew I couldn't risk discovering the truth. Consciously, I knew that escaping, even for a day, was a terrible, horrible, no good, very bad idea.

I wish I could say that after my introvert awakening, I did a better job of meeting my own needs, but I didn't. Being an introvert felt lesser than being an extrovert. Those individuals with huge social circles and endless energy seemed to have all the fun. Extroverts said *yes* to things. Introverts said *no*. No, I'm not going to join, not going to call you, not going to hang out. All those nos made me feel like an outsider.

The Introvert Advantage by Marti Olsen Laney, Psy. D. confirmed I was an "innie," drawing energy from my "internal world of ideas, emotions, and impressions." And it confirmed my experience of early motherhood: "Focusing twenty-four hours a day on the needs of another being can be extraordinarily taxing."

As a child and teen, being an introvert wasn't a problem. With no one to care for but myself, I naturally gravitated toward solitude, spending long hours on my bed devouring books, or painting or drawing. I was fortunate that even in a family of six kids, I could always find a place to be alone. In college, I retreated to the library stacks. After marriage but "BC"—Before

Children—if Mike was out or busy, I was free to read, sew, or nap.

When Mike was around, however, I felt compelled to be on call for him. This was my expectation, not his. When we had unstructured time, I waited to see how he was going to spend it before deciding what I wanted to do. After we had kids, I put myself on call for them. I stopped playing the radio in the house so I could hear them. In the bathroom, I didn't turn on the fan. My motherhood duties overrode my intrinsic need for quiet seclusion.

Another book, Susan Cain's *Quiet*, deepened my self-understanding, and I filled its pages with underlines and sticky notes. Cain mentioned HSPs—Highly Sensitive People—and referenced the work of Dr. Elaine Aron, so I also bought her book, *The Highly Sensitive Person.*

Usually, when someone is described as sensitive, it means empathic (a compliment), or easily offended (a criticism). According to Aron, a research psychologist and psychotherapist, "highly sensitive" refers to an innate trait in which the brain processes subtleties of information, and the nervous system reacts to that information more sensitively than for less sensitive people. I found myself on every page:

> *Overstimulated by intense, complex, chaotic, or novel environments.* For me, that meant loud music, violent movies, big crowds, the kids' sporting events, the never-ending clutter and disarray of house projects.
>
> *Overwhelmed by emotion.* I cried easily with joy, pride, or grief, and in reaction to my personal circumstances, those of others around me, the world at large, or TV commercials. Once, I even

cried over a *Zits* comic in the Sunday paper.

Aware of subtleties. I immediately sensed a person's reaction to me based on their tone of voice, facial expression, and body language. I often used the word "nuance" when searching for the exact word to convey my thoughts. "I'm a flawed mother" feels distinctly different from "I'm a mother with flaws."

Mike and I had misunderstandings over nuance. If I complained about someone at work, he might later refer to "the person you hate," forcing me to clarify. "I don't hate them, I just hated that time they [fill in the blank]." Unable to see the difference, Mike got annoyed.

Often, when he asked my help picking out a tie for work, I'd reject his selection.

"I know you hate red ties," he concluded.

"I don't hate red ties. I hate *that* tie with *that* shirt."

He still didn't get it. One day, he showed me his typical red tie/blue shirt combination.

I made a face. "Don't even show me red ties because you know I hate them."

He laughed, and after we repeated the scenario several times, it finally sank in.

I took the self-assessment test in Aron's book. In addition to being an off-the-chart introvert, I was an off-the-chart HSP. One of the few statements that did not describe me, however, was, "When I was a child, my parents and teachers seemed to see me as sensitive or shy." I circled "False." Then I remembered an episode when I was about eleven.

School was out for the summer. My mother had plans for the day, so she dropped me off with a family friend. I was happy to be there—I loved Mrs. M. and was comfortable with her children, at least within the familiar circle of family gatherings. Shortly after I arrived, a gang of outdoorsy, athletic-looking kids trickled into the house to prepare for a hike. I was neither outdoorsy nor athletic, and hiking included too many unsettling unknowns: people, terrain, expectations.

"I'll just stay here with you," I told Mrs. M.

"No, Karen, you have to go with the kids."

Even at eleven, I got the distinct feeling she had observed a pattern of me choosing the safety of adult company over the rough and tumble play of my peers. I think she relished the opportunity to drag me out of my comfort zone to the place she felt I belonged. Properly chastised, I didn't argue. I dared not make waves. I dared not disappoint a person I loved.

Reluctantly, I trotted along with the adventurers. At one point, a large outcropping of rock blocked our trail, which curved around to a hidden place beyond. The ground below the rock fell away to a deep precipice. One by one, the brave explorers side-stepped along a narrow ledge, grabbed hold of the rock face, and disappeared from view.

I was sure I would fall and sustain grave injuries, even death. Perhaps in reality it was not that dangerous, but to my impressionable, sensitive mind, it was terrifying. Yet, I didn't want to ruin the day for the other kids or risk being called "chicken" or "baby." I took my turn, grasping the rock for dear life, trying not to look over my shoulder. I survived without injury—to my body, at least.

By the time we got back, I had a migraine—the first I remember. I went into the bathroom and cried. When I came out, red-faced, Mrs. M. looked surprised.

"Karen, what's wrong dear?"

"I have a really bad headache. Do you have some aspirin?"

My mother picked me up soon after, and I sobbed the whole way home.

Years later, thinking about the incident made my heart race and my eyes smart. The helplessness felt familiar as a recurrent theme of my childhood.

I called my mom.

"Would you have described me as a sensitive child when I was a kid?'

"Absolutely," she replied in that wise, loving tone that had buffered me through life.

I don't remember when I became aware of the concept of people-pleasing. Perhaps in my high school psychology class, where I learned behavior was categorized as passive, assertive, aggressive, or passive-aggressive. Around the same time, my mother learned the same thing in her educational psychology master's program. We often shared our mutual struggle to be assertive, the only acceptable behavior according to our textbooks.

As an adult, my attempts to be assertive rarely turned out as I'd hoped. A teacher friend at my school chatted and laughed with her colleague in the back of her classroom while I tried to teach my lesson. After it happened a few times, I joked with her privately that it was hard for me to think and asked if she could tone it down. She never spoke to me again. Another friend regularly stood me up at the last minute for social outings. Lacking the courage for a face-to-face conversation, I wrote her what I thought was a lovely letter explaining the difficulty of booking and canceling a babysitter. I asked her to be more considerate. She disappeared from my life.

Once, I sat on the living room floor in the dark, phone receiver in hand, working up the nerve to call a few male acquaintances. They had agreed to help demolish our dilapidated garage in exchange for a backyard barbecue steak dinner. They disappeared before the job was done and reappeared after the steak was cold. Mike was not in the least concerned. But over and over in therapy, I'd been counseled to voice my feelings, so finally, I wiped my sweaty palms on my jeans and dialed.

"Hey, Ricky—I wanted to thank you for your help today."

"No problem."

"But where'd you guys go? We weren't done, and you all disappeared."

"Yeah, we made the rounds," Ricky said, his voice excited. "Tony had a light out on his porch and Paul had to get up on his roof."

"Well, I was a little upset." I squirmed, feeling internal pressure to speak my mind but hating every moment. "We had a fridge full of steaks for you guys, and finally I just had to cook them."

"Yeah—they were great."

He didn't get it and I didn't say it in a way that he would. It was a guy thing, and I should have dropped it. I sat in the dark for a while, hating myself—my sensitivity, my inability to own my anger, my struggle to express it effectively.

Since I knew so little of myself, my friends and family (except my mother) didn't know me either. How could they? When I was around them, I became who they expected me to be.

Yet, my life in many ways was full and happy. Perhaps, like a visually impaired person with a keen sense of hearing, I instinctively maximized my strengths. I lacked interpersonal conflict-resolution skills, but I excelled at group facilitation and public speaking—coveted skills in many industries—and my career trajectory rewarded me accordingly. My need to please meant that people liked me, even if I didn't like all of them in return (which usually escaped my immediate awareness). I refrained from "girlfriend" relationships with women who gabbed on the phone regularly and popped in unannounced, but I had dependable friends who sent birthday wishes and Christmas cards, who asked about Matthew, delivered dinners, shared drinks, and watched Stephen through our crisis.

I often thanked my parents for raising me with common sense. Their values and guidance and example enabled me to make good decisions regarding spouse and family and career and finances. My parents' imperfect but solid marriage, based on mutual respect and love, provided a model that ultimately helped my marriage survive.

The greatest outcomes of my cluelessness about what made me tick were Matthew and Stephen. Had I known early on the degree of my sensitivities, had I known how motherhood would tax me to an almost life-threatening degree, I may have opted out of becoming a mother. If so, mine would have been a simpler, calmer life, perhaps, but without the joy of knowing my sons. I would have missed the greatest lessons the universe had in store for me—the lessons of motherhood.

22

Parented-Out

In September 2000, Matthew started ninth grade, Stephen started fourth, and I started my day with a sore right shoulder. By the end of the month, my arm lost the strength to carry a gallon of milk, and hurt so much, I dropped things unexpectedly. By the end of December, I couldn't hold a cup of coffee in my right hand for more than a few seconds. An orthopedist diagnosed *adhesive capsulitis*, known as frozen shoulder. He said it could last a year.

I was able to move my lower right arm out in front of me, hinged at the elbow like Barney the purple dinosaur. I could hold a paring knife and stir a pot and grip a steering wheel, but not scratch my head. The slightest unexpected flinch such as a sneeze or cough or a pencil slipping from my grasp and my involuntary grab for it gave validation to the expression "the pain dropped me to my knees." It also kept me awake for all but a few hours most nights.

One afternoon at work, my Barney arm throbbed merci-
lessly. I had no classroom lessons or students scheduled for the
rest of the day, so I tried to catch up on paperwork at my desk
but couldn't keep my eyes open. I considered making tea in the
faculty room, but then I'd have to carry the hot mug back to
my office, which might as well have been a mile away. Finally,
I got up, shut my door and sat in my threadbare upholstered
chair with my head back. *Just a few minutes*, I told myself. When
I woke to the commotion of dismissal time, I looked at my
watch and gasped. Two hours had passed. I viciously berated
myself in my head.

When I got home, despite my generous nap, I collapsed on
the loveseat and immediately fell to sleep. The sound of the
front door latch woke me. At fourteen, Matthew took the bus
home more often now. I sat up quickly, gently lifting my Barney
arm from its bed of throw pillows and smoothed my hair with
my good hand.

"Hi Matthew, how was your day?"

"K."

"How's the homework situation?"

"Mmm, the usual, I guess."

"Why don't you get yourself a snack? I'm going to lay here
for a little bit, then I'll come up and help you get started before
I pick up Stephen."

A second grader at my school had recently told me his
mother was often passed out on the couch (drunk, I presumed)
when he came home from school. It wasn't the first time I'd
heard that story nor the first student who'd told it. I didn't
want to be that mom, unable to engage with her children. *Am
I really that different?*

That year, my weight ballooned to the highest it had ever been, pushing me solidly into "obese" on a Body Mass Index chart. If I wasn't clinically depressed again, I certainly was miserable, so I got myself back into counseling. Little by little in my sessions, my unhappiness with Mike surfaced. I didn't have enough distance yet from our brain tumor ordeal to identify exactly what had happened between us, but I questioned staying in my marriage. My therapist suggested Mike join us for a few sessions.

"I know you hate the idea, but will you come, just once or twice?" I asked Mike one night in bed. I couldn't see his face, but when he answered, his voice was steady.

"If this is important to you, Karen, I'll go."

The following week, Mike and I sat stiffly in a high-ceilinged office in a downtown Troy brownstone. My therapist, a late-thirties Jay Leno clone, faced us.

"I feel invisible," I said, turning toward Mike. "I can put on a sexy blouse and perfume and fix my hair perfectly, and you won't even notice. I don't know what to do to get your attention."

I glanced down at my hands and toyed with my wedding ring. I still hadn't told Mike about the vice grip food had on my life, but I had finally confessed my bingeing to him.

Then I looked back up at Mike. "So I just say 'the hell with it', and I go binge."

Mike's eyes glistened, his chin on the verge of trembling. He leaned over and took my hand in both of his, caressing my fingers with his thumbs.

"I love you, Karen. You're beautiful. I've known that from

the day we met." We both sniffed. "I'm sorry I didn't notice you. I'll try to pay more attention."

Not long after, I got home from work after a terrible day that I had described to Mike on the phone. As I stepped in the back door, he reached into the freezer and pulled out a Jim Beam Manhattan—my favorite cocktail. Another time, as I started a tearful work-related rant, he took me by the shoulders and led me to the living room.

"Let's go sit down so you can tell me all about it."

Pulling back from him, I eyed him suspiciously. "Who are you and what have you done with my husband?" We doubled over in laughter.

I told Mike I wanted one passionate kiss a day and for him to tell me I was beautiful three times a week. They weren't hard asks. A kiss is enjoyable. A compliment takes no time. They were easier than requesting that he sweep the kitchen floor or clean up his pile of mail in the living room. Those were inconveniences I'd have to work up my nerve to address. But stating my needs so clearly and emphatically solidified a small piece of my self-esteem. I felt assertive, which felt good.

The following March, my shoulder remained in a deep freeze. At the urging of my therapist and with a note from my doctor, I took two weeks off from work. Having time to think convinced me my life was slowly killing me, and if I didn't make drastic changes, I would suffer a heart attack or be diagnosed with cancer within a year. With time to pay more attention to Matthew's daily schoolwork struggles, I also concluded that

Matthew would never make it through high school unless I became his full-time tutor.

"Thank God. It's about time," Mike said, when I told him I wanted to quit my job at the end of the school year. Living on one income would be a stretch, but we had paid off our mortgage early, and we knew how to be frugal. When I told Matthew about my decision, he said, "You mean I'm gonna have the stay-at-home mom I've always wanted?" Filled with guilt and joy, I pulled him into a hug. "You sure will."

Before the onset of my frozen shoulder, I took evening memoir-writing classes at an arts center in Troy. My scribbled yellow legal pads and computer files multiplied. Finally, I decided to get serious about telling my story. Matthew loved the idea.

After school one Friday, when homework could wait, Matthew sat on the loveseat with me to watch *Oprah*. One of the featured stories was a child's medical crisis, and, as the mother on stage fought for composure, I fought to hold back tears. I pictured Matthew and me one day sitting in the deep leather chairs, Oprah and the audience riding our rollercoaster with us. Holding in my pain, I said nothing.

Matthew turned toward me. "Mom, we could be on *Oprah*."

I looked at him—my brave, determined son, rolling his wrists and cracking his knuckles. I kissed him on the cheek. "You read my mind."

But how would our story end? Would I ever be able to write, "Then Matthew got better"? Later that month, we emailed his surgeon:

Beginning in December 2000, Matthew began experiencing more difficulty than usual with concentration and short-term memory. These symptoms gradually worsened. By early March, his grades and mood dropped significantly as a result. [A psychiatrist is evaluating Matthew] for these symptoms, as well as for facial and motor tics…We feel that the changes…warrant an early MRI [sooner than scheduled].

Dr. Gordinsky approved the MRI, which showed that Matthew's tumor had not grown and the ETV was working. I felt the familiar battle of emotions—relief that nothing was going wrong and dread that nothing was going right. It affirmed my decision to leave my job.

After Mike drove away with the boys that first school morning in September, Matthew in tenth grade, Stephen in fifth, I sipped my coffee at the kitchen table, wrapped in silence. The quiet reminded me of my first day back to work at the library after Matthew was born, when the hushed lobby was a refuge. Fourteen years later, I wondered if I could ever get enough quiet to make up for the years of tumult. I smiled, remembering when I was a kid and believed, like many children, that if you dug a hole deep enough, you'd pop out on the opposite side of the world. My hole of need felt that deep, and during the days ahead, I slowly filled it with naps, solitude, and long walks.

On September 11, I drove to my old school to help orient my new replacement as I had volunteered to do. The car radio announced that a small plane had hit a building in New York City. I didn't think much about it. I was too excited to see the students and staff, to soak in the joy of the legacy I'd left without buckling under the demands of the job.

Moments after I sat down with the new counselor, she was called into a crisis meeting. As I walked toward the exit, I passed classrooms with TVs playing, horrified at the images, aghast that children were being exposed to the carnage. *The students will need me,* I thought as I left, knowing it was no longer my job to help them.

I sobbed on the way home and sat glued to the TV for the rest of the day. I had comfort knowing the student who needed me most—the child for whom I would sacrifice everything—finally was to have my full attention. I picked up the kids from school early, listened to their fears, and reassured them as best as I could that our family was safe. Then my late-shift job with Matthew began.

To reinforce what Matthew should have learned in school, I created my own whole-body teaching style. Equal parts strategy, performance, and fun, I did whatever I could to stick facts to Matthew's Teflon brain. I danced to the rhythm of science facts, sang algebra formulas, and pranced like a cheerleader to world history battles and dates. The more silly, the more memorable. If Matthew laughed, all the better. I taught him about mnemonic devices, and we created them by the dozens. For example, if the ideas spread by imperialism were political, economic, environmental, or social, the mnemonic would be PEES, as in "Peese don't take over my country."

Most of Matthew's teachers respected his 504 accommodations and trusted our judgment in limiting homework. A few were less supportive. "Some boys try to get away with as little work as possible," one teacher said at a conference. Another wrote on a report card, "He does not spend adequate time preparing." Still, with the help of several consultant teachers and the bump in grades from his jazz band, Matthew passed each semester, even making honor roll multiple times.

Matthew turned sixteen three weeks before his junior year and asked to get his learner's permit. One night, I took my turn in the hot seat while Matthew drove to his job at a pizza parlor. He had wanted to work part time, and a few hours one school night per week felt reasonable—if we both survived the ten-block commute. First, we sat in the driveway for a few minutes until I reminded him to start the car. Then he got in the wrong lane—again—at a familiar intersection. The previous week, he forgot how to get to work altogether, although the trip only required two turns. One of his tics at that time was to crane his head from side to side, so when he craned left, the car drifted left. When he craned right, the car drifted right until I yelled, "Matthew, you're drifting!"

On straight roads, Matthew drove well under the speed limit. When he approached a curve, he accelerated, and I braced my arms against the dashboard. He couldn't seem to undo the momentum, his left tires rolling over the yellow lines or his right tires grinding over the shoulder, while I pumped invisible brakes. "Slow down, Matthew!"

Mike had taught Matthew to glance both ways when passing through an intersection to be sure no cars had run a light or stop sign. Matthew's interpretation of "glance" was to stop in the middle of the crossroads, get a good long look one way and then a good long look the other way, while I yelled, "Don't stop! Go, go go!" I asked Mike to unteach Matthew so I could reteach him. But Matthew couldn't understand what he was doing wrong and continued his dangerous habit while I freaked out in the passenger seat. Later, I learned a symptom of brain-injury is perseveration—getting stuck in a behavior or on an idea. "Stuck" described us both.

When Matthew had accumulated enough supervised driving hours to take his road test, I expected him to fail. I hoped he would; he wasn't safe on the road. I believed his brain tumor would forever deny him this rite of passage, and I imagined breaking the news gently to him. What a blow that would be. But Matthew passed on the first try. (Almost thirty years earlier, it had taken me three tries, one of which involved losing control of the car and plowing into a snowbank.) Unable to control fate, I let go.

Fate validated me when Matthew had a few accidents. After one three-car pile-up, he called to tell me, and I was so mad at him for his poor driving skills, instead of asking, *Are you okay?* I demanded, through gritted teeth, "Where are you?" When I arrived on the scene a few miles from home, I felt relieved to see there were no injuries, although Mike's car was totaled. The accident was clearly Matthew's fault—he had turned left into oncoming (and, fortunately, slow-moving) traffic.

One of the other drivers was incredibly gracious, although her brand new cherry red SUV had significant damage. The third driver was equally pleasant despite being about-to-drop-pregnant. I apologized to her on behalf of my son and asked if she was okay. I suspect she may have been driving without a license or had some other reason to not make waves, as the police officer kept her in his patrol car for an unusually long time. If she lost her baby, her suffering would eclipse ours, but the emotional and financial toll on Matthew and our family would be devastating. We were lucky—Matthew got off with a ticket, our insurance jumped but didn't soar, and we never heard from the pregnant lady, who I pray had a healthy delivery.

We had passed Matthew's fifth year of recovery, the milepost after which children with brain damage supposedly won't continue to improve. I wondered if this was as good as it was going to get.

In August, we took a weeklong vacation in the Pocono Mountains with my extended family, all eighteen of us under one large roof. A week after we returned, my youngest brother emailed me his unsolicited impressions:

> *It's hard for me to say this, but despite all the progress Matthew has made, he still strikes me as slow, both physically and mentally. In the midst of a couple of conversations, he would appear to be dazed and miss the point but then it was as if you could see the light bulb go on and he was back and capable of grasping the whole conversation and responding in an intelligent way.*
>
> *And every time we went to leave the house, he seemed to lose track of any number of things: shoes, towel, glasses, shirt, and while there are many people that misplace things, it seems to be chronic and pervasive with him.*
>
> *Seeing all this I had to control myself to not get mad*

at him and when I thought of having to deal with that
every day, it made me quite sympathetic to both of you.

Feeling understood was a balm. At first glance, Matthew appeared perfectly fine, just a quirky teen with a few tics. Spend a little time with him, and you'd notice Alzheimer's-like symptoms—lucid one moment, lost the next. Spend a day with him, and you'd want to tear out your hair.

Matthew would be a senior in a few weeks. The following year, if all went well, he would leave for college. Was it even possible? I wanted him to believe it was, despite my doubts. At the same time, I had to believe it, because I didn't know how much longer I could live with him.

In May 2004, Matthew made me a believer. He graduated from high school, received the Louis Armstrong Jazz Award, and got admitted to an out-of-town college.

"I'm finally doing a retreat!" I told my mother later that summer. My bed for the five-day writing getaway lay in a dusty communal room with no A/C or fan. The bright light outside the window gave me a view each sleepless night of a colony of bats swooping into a swarm of bugs. Each day, tufts of condensation rose from the lake, filling the air and my lungs with what felt like mold.

For two suffocating days, I wrote and revised, listened and learned. Writing my story felt new and raw, but of course, I lingered in the thick of it, living my experience every day. On the third afternoon, my introvert needs kicked in, and I escaped by myself to dip my bare feet in the lake. A small patch of grass next to the water beckoned me, and I tiptoed in, sat down, and took off my sandals. Gingerly, I put one foot and then the other in the icy water, pulling them in and out until they adjusted. Then I opened my yellow legal pad, took out a pencil, flicked an ant from my shorts, and wrote:

> *Matthew leaves for college in 1 month. What the hell am I doing here? I should be home cherishing every moment with him before he grows up completely. But many moments with Matthew are not cherish-able. They are frustrating. They are reminders of the progress that eludes him.*

> *Maybe with him at college, I will forget he is sick. Maybe I can pretend he has finally recovered for good. Or at least that he has developed whatever coping skills he will need to make the most of his many assets. So he will stop relying on me to cope for him.*

> *But I will also worry. Not so much about him, but how others will respond to him. Will they see the charming, gentle soul that is the heart of Matthew, or will they see someone slightly odd? Will they think he's deceitful or confused?*

Small groups of women occasionally strolled along the path behind me, laughing and chatting, but I kept my head down. I was tired of my story. I wanted a different tale, one where the mother was sad to see her firstborn leave for college. That mother's heart would ache. She would cry to her friends, The years flew by. I want to do it all over again! I wanted to be that mother telling that story.

With a vise constricting my heart, I wrote one final entry:

Today, I am parented-out with Matthew. There is nothing left to give. I can't worry anymore. I can't watch over him anymore. I'm done.

Suffocating from the heat, humidity, and weight of my story, I hurried back to my room and packed my bag. Maybe I shouldn't have rushed back to the life that wore me out, but I had to escape the story of it.

I didn't write again for years.

23

Freedom at Last

I felt all but invisible walking away from the moment I had
dreamed of for eighteen years. The hallway bustled with students and parents, mini refrigerators, desktop computers, and
laundry bags. Mike and Stephen followed me out of the building, but not Matthew. With hugs and kisses and well-wishes,
we had left him alone in his dorm room.

Matthew was an incoming freshman in 2004 at the State
University of New York at Oneonta, ninety minutes southwest
of Troy. He chose to major in music industry, a degree we all
believed would be more marketable than music performance.
I simply wanted him to get a college degree, preferably a bach-
elors. He had many strikes against him, but a four-year degree
might at least get him on first base. We had ruled out learning a
trade like auto mechanic or HVAC installer because, other than
drumming, Matthew wasn't good with his hands; he wasn't a
tinkerer. He needed to rely on his brain, as compromised as it

was.

Mike drove us home and Stephen rode shotgun while I crouched in the back seat and cried the whole way. Scenes of the previous eighteen years flashed before my eyes. Since the day I had pushed Matthew into the world, he had pushed me to the brink of what I thought I could survive. At that moment, though, I felt no joy or peace or sense of accomplishment. Depleted, barely able to muster the strength to feel numb, I cried from sheer exhaustion.

When we got home, I wandered into Matthew's room, lay on his bed, and shed a few more tears. His room still had the astronaut border, the bright yellow walls, the blue built-in desk. When Matthew was ten, we'd bought him glow-in-the-dark star stickers, which he applied to his ceiling in the shape of constellations. They hung there still, awaiting darkness to share their light. The room was a happy room, despite the difficult memories, and I couldn't help but smile.

Rolling to my back, I inhaled deeply, and serenity found me. I had given Matthew my all. Now it was up to him.

Mike and I had encouraged Matthew to take advantage of 504 accommodations and support services at Oneonta like he had at La Salle, but he refused. I didn't blame him—college was his chance to leave behind who he had been in high school, a chance to see himself differently, to blend in rather than stand out.

The new Matthew surprised me when I picked him up for the Columbus Day break. I pulled up to his dorm, but the only kid there, sitting on the steps, had an adorable mop of blond, curly hair. My heart sank with memories of walking the halls at La Salle in search of my brown-haired son among all the other boys with the same, short haircut. Then the blond kid waved to me. *It was Matthew.* He looked like the coolest, cutest freshman ever.

The world is full of judgment, full of first impressions made in a tenth of a second, according to research. In that split second, Matthew's tics and mannerisms made him vulnerable to bullying and teasing. For a brief time in high school, a couple of boys picked on him, but one call to Brother Chris stopped it immediately. In college, no big brother was going to come to the rescue, and I hoped looking cool would offer Matthew some level of protection.

When I picked him up for the Thanksgiving break, orange was his new blond, a result of a botched attempt to return to his darker roots. When he got in the car, a glint of light flashed from his earlobe.

My gauge for judging teen experimentation is its impact on health and wellness. Matthew's hair color was a nonissue; it would grow out. I wasn't happy about how he'd acquired his piercing—a guy down the hall with a needle and a potato—but his earlobe didn't look infected. Mike wasn't as amused about Matthew's new bling, fearing tattoos, practically a crime in his book, were next. But tattoos never materialized, nor did additional piercings, and Matthew stuck to his natural hair from then on.

The first year Matthew was away, I committed to *not* keeping busy, other than chauffeuring Stephen to school and extracurricular activities. Then life quickly filled the void. I started a business designing and installing perennial gardens, a back-breaking venture with little return on investment that lasted only one season. Our pastor tapped me to run our church's religious education program, a part-time position I kept until our parish closed three years later. In the meantime, on a walk through our neighborhood one day, I was struck by the junk-filled yards, hanging gutters, and peeling paint of an alarming number of homes. Mike and I decided to move across town, so we cleaned out twenty years of clutter and finished all the DIY projects we had not yet finalized.

Over the years, Matthew had often asked, "Mom, when do you think you and Dad will have the house done?"

My customary answer: "By the time you go to college," which proved to be a fairly accurate prediction.

Matthew had some of the typical bumps of campus life—roommate conflicts, questionable friends, a few course mix-ups, and a failed accounting class, which he made up over the summer. Every May, we'd readjusted to living under the same roof, and every September, I was sad but relieved when he left.

He passed all his courses in four years, and I shook my head in amazement. In May 2008, his only remaining requirement was a two-credit, unpaid internship, which he arranged with a music studio in Ithaca, NY, another ninety minutes west from Oneonta. For two months, he'd live alone in a city where he knew no one.

During the years of parenting Matthew, I'd had a broad knowledge base to help him grow up. I knew that carrots were healthy and Twinkies were not, that clothes left in the dryer would wrinkle, that grandmothers love phone calls. I knew to turn off lights when you left a room, to show up on time for work, and to keep an extra set of car keys handy. School reports, job interviews, college application essays, even attending a college where I didn't know a soul—I had done it all. In addition to practical skills, I also had wisdom to impart: *Everybody makes mistakes; what matters is how you recover. All your feelings are okay; it's what you do with them that counts. Every person deserves to be treated with respect.*

Although I worried about Matthew being away at college, a campus is a ready-made community. For resident students, potential friends are as close as the four walls of your dorm room and no farther away than across the hall. An older and wiser RA is always on call. I'm not naïve enough to think every student sails through academic life, but on campus, someone nearby likely has your back.

What I'd never done is live alone. I moved from home to college to roommates to Mike. When Matthew moved to Ithaca, I had no benefit of experience with which to guide him.

I felt unmoored with my son living by himself in a strange city, less a lack of faith in Matthew's abilities than my own, but Matthew approached his internship as an adventure. He called home his second night there after he'd walked around town, found an ice cream shop, and listened to a band in the park. I pictured him licking a vanilla cone, soaking up the vibes of independence. On subsequent calls, though, it became clear that what the music studio wanted in an intern was a grunt to haul and set up heavy equipment for summer concerts. Eager to please as always, Matthew scrambled to comply. But the fast-paced, unfamiliar, unstructured environment, the hundred-pound speakers, and the barked orders of his helicopter boss were a checklist for disaster.

Matthew complained of long, hot days and a litany of miscommunications and misunderstandings. His emotional and physical fatigue bled through the phone wires. "That sounds terrible," I said. "I'm so sorry, Matthew."

But I knew how easily those miscommunications happened and that Matthew was often at least partially to blame. I didn't know how to broach that subject, though, without making him feel bad. At the same time, I wanted to scream at the concert crew, *Help him out, you jerks!* Or chastise his boss, *You're getting free labor, what's your problem?*

Matthew stuck it out until the boss and his minions started berating him daily. Quitting was the right decision, yet my hopes deflated to see his future falling apart when his diploma dangled just out of reach. Mike and I made plans to drive out to Oneonta, help Matthew pack up, and come home. We talked about where he might find another internship; Troy wasn't exactly brimming with possibilities.

The next day, Matthew called.

"Hi Mom. I'm at school."

"You mean Oneonta?"

"Yeah, I called my advisor who said he'll let me intern in the summer music program on campus. He found me a dorm room, too."

Huh? Not only had Matthew made the arrangements on his

own, but he had also packed his car by himself and driven back to Oneonta without getting lost. It was an awakening for me— that Matthew might function better when he made his own decisions than when Mike or I made decisions for him.

With the internship completed and his degree granted, Matthew came home. As his belongings spilled from his boxes and bins, his confusion spilled back into our daily lives. Simple chores I asked Matthew to do like unloading the dishwasher, taking out the trash, or switching the laundry from the washer to the dryer were bungled. I simplified each task, wrote down the steps, left him a note. He still got it wrong. Or he'd forget. My standards weren't unreasonably high, but there had to be some level of expectation, didn't there?

"Matthew, we always seem to have these miscommunications," I said after a particularly disastrous chore. "What do you think is going on?"

"I don't…I feel…ahhh…" he began, alternately slapping his hands against his thighs and turning them palms-up. Finally, he gave up. I hated to revert to guessing his thoughts, but my patience was limited.

"Is part of it that you don't want your mother telling you what to do?"

"Yup."

I got it. He hated living at home with his parents. He hated his mother telling him what to do. I hated it, too, but what was the solution? Self-determination might have been Matthew's preferred modus operandi, but neither Mike nor I were ready to hand over the reins of our household to our twenty-one-year-old son.

Matthew returned to the part-time deli job he had held in high school, and I got the bright idea to pay him for odd jobs around the house to supplement his minimum-wage income. My hope was to supplant the parent/child dynamic with a boss/worker one. I thought it might be a win-win—he earns money, we cross things off our to-do list. But no matter how clear and simple Mike or I tried to make an instruction, verbal or written, Matthew didn't get it. The more Matthew botched a job, the more detailed our instructions were the next time. The more we micromanaged a task, the less capable Matthew became.

One assignment he agreed to do was to finish painting a bedroom.

"Try not to get paint on the trim because it's already done," I said, running my hand along the smooth, white finish.

Matthew nodded.

"And I did all the cutting in. See—I gave you about a foot around the windows and doors."

His eyes focused elsewhere.

"See, Matthew" I tapped the wall until his eyes focused there. "All you have to do is to roll the center part of each wall with the tan color."

He nodded.

"So try really hard not to get paint on the trim because it was a lot of work to get a nice, crisp edge."

"Okay, Mom."

That night, I inspected his work. The rolled walls looked fine, but the trim was dotted with dried, tan smears. I ranted to Mike, and when Matthew got home from the deli, I pointed out the problem. He got defensive. It was the roller's fault or the rolling pan or me not being clear. We argued for a few minutes, then I dropped it. *He has a brain tumor.*

Mike and I often disagreed about the level of difficulty of a chore and whether Matthew could complete it. Mike's expectations were higher; mine were lower, a decades-old pattern, and I hated that we were bickering again about how to parent our son. What we did agree on was the need to be less forgiving about the quality of work for paid jobs. If Matthew were ever to get and keep decent employment, he had to learn how to follow directions. When Mike or I pointed that out to Matthew or told him where a task had failed and what needed to be corrected, his face turned dark, his shoulders sagged. Often, he blamed us for the miscommunication.

I tried to talk with Matthew about how his brain tumor and lingering hydrocephalus affected his skills. "It's not your fault, Matthew," I said. "It's your brain tumor." *You are separate from your condition,* I wanted him to know. *Your brain tumor does not define you.*

He refused to discuss it.

I gently introduced the word "disability" into family conversations, hoping Matthew would follow through on my suggestions for getting support. Mike refused to go there, as did Matthew.

But it didn't matter how Mike or I spoke about what was going on, or if we did, because Matthew was an adult now. It was his decision to accept help or not.

At Matthew's college graduation ceremony in the height of the 2008 recession, I had looked down at the mass of black mortarboards, knowing they constituted a speck in the ocean of graduates across the country. Where would they all find jobs? Would Matthew? Would I?

The previous year, I had started to think about returning to work. Stephen had his driver's license, worked part-time, and played trumpet in the La Salle jazz band. A good student and independent, he needed little attention from me. With time to focus on myself, I decided for the gazillionth time to lose weight. However, I approached it differently than before. For starters, I stopped weighing myself, judging my progress not by the number on the scale but on what I ate and how active I was each day. I used a lunch plate for dinner to control serving sizes, and filled it with vegetables, lean protein, and whole grains, in that order. I drank water by the quart. For exercise, I set a goal so small, I couldn't say no to it: ten minutes three times per week. That quickly grew in frequency and duration because it felt so good. Then I bought a set of dumbbells and worked out at home, building muscle to burn more calories. Over the year, I lost thirty pounds. More significantly, *I lost the urge to binge.* Not completely, but enough that for the first time in my adult life, I controlled food, not the other way around.

I made a conscious decision to become the trendy, put-together professional woman I had always envisioned. My hair stylist cut my long hair into a chic reverse bob, shorter in the back than in front, with chunky lowlights and highlights. When I shopped for new clothes, I asked myself who was more likely to wear a piece—my mom or my younger sister. If the answer was "Mom," I put the item back on the rack.

268

My job hunting yielded an underpaid position at a breast cancer not-for-profit, a reprieve from the stress at home, and a steppingstone to regain my foothold in the job market. When my twenty-five-year-old colleague came to work one day in white jeans and a lime green flouncy top almost identical to mine, I knew I'd nailed the look I wanted.

Matthew and I shared job-hunting resources, bonding over the slim pickings. He wrote textbook-perfect cover letters, had good eye contact, a big smile, and a solid handshake, and his few lingering tics were subtle and sporadic. His interviews often resulted in job offers. But his struggle to remember and follow directions, pay attention, and stay organized—executive functioning skills—made it difficult to perform his duties. Soon after he started, he was let go or pressured to quit.

The psychologist who performed Matthew's post-college neuropsychological evaluation warned of this. A young person like Matthew with a "borderline impairment" may succeed in college, with its structure of course schedules and syllabi and tests. But the relative freedom and sometimes unclear expectations of a job may be his undoing.

Thus began a revolving door of Matthew's low-wage, part-time jobs, at least a dozen over the next eighteen months, none of which lasted more than a few months, many of which ended badly. In one year alone, he held at least nine jobs. Census taker. Phone book deliverer. Temp office worker. Aflac salesperson. Sales associate at Casual Male and Metro Mattress. Mall positions at Macy's, Lindt Chocolates, and Tea World. Delivery person at Rent-A-Center, resulting in his most infamous firing after he dropped a couch in the mud.

In the midst of his career drama, Matthew approached Mike

and me one night. His face was flushed, his tics pronounced.

"I'm moving out," he said.

"What?" I sputtered, as my heart did a flip. It wasn't a happy flip, despite my long-held dream of independence for Matthew and space for myself. It was an *Oh no!* flip of impending disaster. *You can't afford it! You can't manage it! How will I get to you if there's an emergency?*

"Yeah," he said. "My friend from grade school-his parents have an apartment for rent about five minutes from here. I gave them a security deposit. We're moving in this weekend."

I pressed my hands together in front of my mouth like I was praying and looked back and forth from son to husband.

"This is a big step, Matthew," Mike said. "How will you afford it?"

Matthew's face brightened, his posture straightened. "It's $300 a month," he said. "I know I'm not making much at my part-time jobs, but I'll have enough."

I took a deep breath. By this time, I had left the breast cancer agency for a worksite health promotion position at a health insurance company. There, I helped employers implement programs and policies to improve the health of their workforces. At fifty-one, for the first time in my life, I made good money. In fact, when I hung up the phone after receiving the offer, I literally sank to my knees, floored by my good fortune. I could have floated to the ceiling from the weight lifted—my fear that Mike and I would be unable to support Matthew financially when he needed it.

I hugged and congratulated Matthew on his pending move, reminding myself we'd be okay.

Matthew's departure emptied our nest, at least during the

school year, when Stephen attended Syracuse University for electrical engineering. He had gotten sullen and testy during his high school years, so when we dropped him off at college, I had the familiar guilt about my relief, the familiar tearful ride home, the familiar serenity that followed.

I relished the freedom, and Mike and I enjoyed our new-found time as a couple. To celebrate our 30th anniversary in September 2012, we took our first trip to Europe, cruising down the Danube River. Having eschewed cable TV when the kids were young, we treated ourselves to Dish TV, and promptly got sucked into *Monk* and *Everyone Loves Raymond* reruns (neither of which we'd seen the first time around), and later, the reality TV series *Breaking Amish*. We learned to snowshoe, thawing out in the evening in front of the fireplace with a drink. On summer evenings, we practically lived on our deep front porch. Our nest didn't feel empty; it felt spacious.

Every few months, Matthew called and said, "I have to talk. Can I come over?" We never knew if it would be another girl who dumped him or another lost job. Grateful he turned to us, I was happy to be his confidante yet relieved when he returned to his own space. After each urgent phone call or visit, I worried that the current crisis would break Matthew's spirit. Each time, I worried about self-harm. And each time, Matthew proved me wrong. Although he got frustrated and discouraged, he grew from the experience and the next day went out to try again. He never gave up.

Throughout this time, I tried ever-so-gently to push the idea of him getting help with his difficulties (I had stopped using the word "disability"), and every time, Matthew declined. But one day, unbeknownst to me, he had called one of the agency numbers I gave him and applied for career counseling.

Then, like a rusty pendulum clock coming back to life, everything started to tick. Each cog of every gear in his brain nudged the next one until the machine that was Matthew began to purr.

Part 4

24

Living with a Poltergeist

"If you want a beer, Matt," I yelled from the living room, "Dad has some in the fridge."

Eighteen years after his diagnosis and surgery, Matt joined me on the couch one Saturday afternoon with a Saranac IPA. At twenty-nine, he sported a neatly trimmed beard and trendy long-on-top messy hair. Occasionally, he wiggled his lips, his only discernible tic remaining.

He pulled a two-inch blue binder from his backpack, his face aglow.

"What's this?" I asked.

"It's my career binder. I'm reading *What Color Is Your Parachute* and taking notes. I want to run some things by you."

As he flipped through to find the section he wanted, I saw page after page of handwritten notes representing hours of work. I didn't find words to respond right away, but I sat back and looked at him, my eyebrows lifted, lips pressed together in a look that said *Holy Moly*.

"I'm impressed, Matt." (I said that to him a lot lately.) "I owned that book when I got out of college, but I never completed a single assignment. I didn't think *anyone* completed the assignments!" He laughed.

Matt gave his beard exaggerated strokes as he often did to pantomime deep contemplation. Then he found the page he wanted and launched into an animated analysis of his core values, problem-solving style, and preferred worksite environment. He rattled off the list of professionals, including former teachers and counselors, with whom he'd networked. Mesmerized, I hardly paid attention to the details. *He has a brain tumor. He has a brain tumor. He has a brain tumor.*

Matthew's parachute had a rainbow of options. Maybe the hues were less vibrant than for other young adults, maybe the chute wouldn't open as wide or carry him as far, but when it held him aloft, the joy in my heart filled the skies.

Sitting back, Matt took a swig of beer.

"Matt, can I ask you something? But tell me if you don't want to discuss it."

"Sure, Mom."

"What made you finally decide to embrace your disability and get help?" I didn't expect him to have a clear answer. I didn't think he'd had an *aha* moment.

"It was the Metro Mattress job," he said without pause. "Do you remember that list of mattresses I had to memorize?"

I remembered. It was sometime in 2010, his turnstile year of jobs. He got the sales position easily and the manager handed him a multi-page list of "extra firm," "memory core," and "inner spring" mattresses to be memorized within three days. Matt had asked me for help, and I gave it my best mnemonic ingenuity, but our efforts were unsuccessful, and he was let go.

"When I couldn't memorize that list, I realized something wasn't right." Matt folded and unfolded his hands. "That's when I filled out that ACCESS-VR application."

Willing my brain to tease out memories, I remembered telling Matt about ACCESS-VR, a vocational rehabilitation program, after he had graduated from college. But he had ignored it for several years. When he finally did complete and submit his application, I thought it was only to get me off his back. I didn't know then that Metro Mattress had been his rock bottom.

His ACCESS-VR counselor helped Matt realize he worked best in a structured, predictable, calm environment with regular hours. The agency had no luck in finding him a suitable job, and eventually hired him as a receptionist in one of their offices. His performance reviews were poor his first year, his supervisors unhelpful. Even working for a rehab agency, success eluded him. Once, he mixed up a photocopying task so badly, someone else had to take over. I remember thinking, *My college-educated son has trouble mastering the art of photocopying. Is this as far as he'll go?* He finally got the hang of the job, but his position was cut in 2013. I got all *woe is me.* Matt simply moved on.

He took a customer liaison position in the high-pressure body shop of a busy car dealership, a bad fit from the start. Then, one day, he parked a customer's car—a standard transmission, which he had never driven—and nearly burned out the clutch. Fortunately, the manager had taken a liking to him and moved him into the business office as a scan tech.

"What's a scan tech?" I had asked him, thinking it must involve more than simply scanning documents. It did, requiring organizational skills beyond his ability. Again, I lamented his challenges. Again, he stuck it out until he mastered the job, refusing to let his tumor hold him back. Then he readied his parachute, secured his harness, and prepared for his next adventure.

I returned to the present, Matt sitting across from me in the living room.

"Matt, I have another question."

He closed his binder and set it on the coffee table.

"I don't remember asking you when you were a kid what was going on. I didn't think you'd know. Were you aware that things were getting harder for you?"

"I remember when I gave up."

My heart lurched.

"I was in fourth grade. This kid in my class was doing long division at the blackboard. He wasn't a great student, but he was getting all the problems correct. But I was lost. I remember thinking, 'That should be me up there. That's *my* place.'"

Matt's face dropped. I wanted to reach back in time, grab that fourth grade Matthew and hold him. Tell him I'd walk with him through what was to come. That he'd find his place again.

"Matt, I'm so sorry you felt that way. I'm so sorry I didn't know, that I never asked."

"I don't think I'd have said anything," Matt answered. "I couldn't explain it."

We both sat for a moment, lost in our thoughts.

"And, when you and Dad got frustrated with me, I just saw it as a big joke."

This admission brings me comfort.

"That explains it, Matt. You were so silly. Most of the time, you seemed happy."

He smiled, as did I.

Matt's tumor was a mischievous poltergeist, quiet and in hiding much of the time, waiting until that moment it was forgotten. Then, sneaking up from behind, it brazenly knocked us upside the head with a *thwack! I'm here, I'm here, remember me?* Its favorite game was toying with Matt's sense of time. Days, dates, hours, yesterdays, last weeks, tomorrows—all were fair game. Even when Matt entered a commitment in his phone, he might enter it incorrectly or forget to check it. And if the date changed? The poltergeist had a field day, firing Matt's neurons into a labyrinth of possibilities.

In August the following year, I had just finished transplanting daylilies in the backyard when Mike pulled up after running some errands.

"I guess you've been busy," he said, picking a piece of mulch from my hair.

Simultaneously, our cell phones jingled. It was a text from Matt at 5:50 p.m.

I'm leaving now. r u still coming?

Mike and I looked at each other in a panic. The week before, Matt had invited us to the thirtieth birthday dinner his girlfriend planned for him. The dinner was the next day, Sunday, at 6 p.m.

"Omigod, do you think Matt's referring to his birthday dinner?" I said.

Mike and I checked our phones. Sure enough, the earlier text had said Sunday.

I called Matt.

"Matt, where are you going and why do you ask if we're coming?"

"Um, well, didn't I tell you about my birthday dinner?"

"Yes, but you told us it was tomorrow. Sunday!"

"I di—? Are you su—? Wait, what's today? Hold on."

I waited.

"Ooooh, yeah, I guess I did." He laughed nervously. "I'm sorry."

I laughed, too, because living with a brain tumor makes you prioritize what's important.

"I've been gardening, so I'll have to shower, but we'll be there as soon as we can."

I hung up and threw my hands in the air. "Someday I'll kill him!" Then I raced inside to shower.

This type of thing happened. All. The. Time.

He has a brain tumor. He has a brain tumor. He has a brain tumor.

We learned to laugh. Living with Matt's brain tumor greased our backs so little inconveniences slid off more easily.

The poltergeist toyed with us in frightening ways, too. At 3:30 one winter morning, our house phone rang. I jumped out of bed to get it, and the moment my eyes focused on the number, it went dead. "I think that was Matt," I said. Mike sat up and fumbled for his cell phone, then I heard my phone ring down-stairs and ran down to catch it on the fourth ring.

"Matt, what's up?"

"I'm at the hospital." He chuckled.

"Okay..." His laugh gave me permission to be calm for the moment.

"I got up a few hours ago and felt a little dizzy, so I went into the kitchen to get a glass of water."

As Matt talked, I scooted back upstairs and put the phone on speaker.

"You okay, Matt?" Mike called when I entered the room.

"Yeah, Dad. So, I noticed that a knob on the stove was turned on a little. I turned it off right away and opened a window, but then I got so dizzy and disoriented, I didn't know what room I was in. I mean, I knew I was in my apartment, but..." His voice got hushed. "I didn't know what room I was in."

Mike and I had been regarding each other warily. Now, our eyes widened. Two years before, Matt had moved from his apartment with noisy friends to his own place. It had only four rooms.

"When I finally found my way back to the bedroom," Matt continued, "I thought I was going to pass out, so I called 911."

I pictured him lying on the floor, not having called in time, but I made myself focus on his words. The EMTs had tested the room for natural gas and carbon monoxide, but the open window had already cleared the air. His blood tests at the hospital were negative, so he was waiting to get discharged and would need a ride home. I had a million questions, but they could wait.

"I'm on my way, Matt."

"Karen, I'll go." Mike flung off his covers. But I insisted. Mike was in the middle of his busy season at work, and I had no commitments on my calendar that day. It reminded me of the years when Matt was a baby, and I refused Mike's help. This time, though, when I got back home, I'd have the house to myself and could climb into bed to recover. I'd finally learned the importance of self-care.

In the emergency room hallway, crowded with wheelchairs and IV poles, I found Matt sitting up in a hospital bed, his pajamaed legs dangling over the side, his winter boots on but untied. I leaned over to kiss him on the forehead and pulled up a chair to wait for his discharge.

Matt confided that he'd woken disoriented a few times before when the burners were not a factor. "I'm a little concerned," he said. "I wonder if something's going on with the tumor."

So it was on his radar, too. I was naive to think it wouldn't be; it would always be on our family's radar. But we rarely talked about his tumor. The more secure Matt got in his independent life, the less he wanted to acknowledge his past. I respected that, keeping my worries to myself.

Matt followed up with his neurologist and got the all-clear. We never did figure out what had caused the episodes of disorientation. But, like beating cancer, living with a brain tumor comes with the knowledge that an invisible war could be waging at any moment. And yet Matt kept winning the battles.

Since the day Matt graduated from college, our dream for him had been a job with New York State—Mike's employer—providing benefits, retirement, and opening thousands of doors. The competition for those jobs was fierce. When Matt finally embraced his disability, Mike accepted it, too, and he discovered a 55b designation for people with disabilities, exempting them from the civil service exam requirement. Matt's application was approved, but he took the civil service exams anyway.

He made it to the second round of interviews for a phone support job at the bottom rung of the state pay scale. But it was still an "in" to the system. He had earned the interview on his own merit, without mentioning 55b.

For two weeks, I heard nothing from Matt about the interview, so finally, I texted him.

Did u hear back yet about the job?
Yes
Yes?
Yes i got the job

I called him. "Matt, you got the job?"
"Yup."
I tried not to scream. As he filled in the details, I heard pride, relief, satisfaction in his voice. Did he hear the same in mine?

His patience and professionalism helped Matt excel, and he became a valued member of the team. I felt myself slowly decompress, as if every cell in my body, one-by-one, let out a satisfied *aaah*. I had made it. *We* had made it.

As Matt cemented his career, mine dissolved, complications of decades-long IBS soon forcing me to resign. I resented the irony of being a Wellness Director too sick to work. At fifty-seven, I wasn't ready to retire. I loved my job, loved helping people improve their lives, and loved that bi-weekly deposit in my bank account. At first, I was distraught, then I realized the universe had given me a gift: time to finish my book.

The unstructured hours also gave me time to reflect on my journey. I wondered who I'd have been had motherhood been easy. Self-righteous was one answer. When Matt skipped over the terrible twos, before he hit his horrible fours, I had a glimpse of that mother. *See how well I parent my child. See how well he behaves and performs and achieves. Look to me to see how motherhood is done right.* That mother would have been disgustingly disagreeable. I would have hated her, as would other moms. Adversity had kept me humble, and I was grateful for the lesson.

A less demanding motherhood also would have kept me clueless about my Achilles heel: people-pleasing. At some point, would I have realized the world wouldn't treat me with kid gloves just because I feared conflict? Would I somehow have learned to speak up for myself? I had broken through my wall of agreeableness enough to get Matt diagnosed, but the dismantling of my self stopped while I threw my energy into his recovery. For twenty years, I retreated into the shadow of my own barricade. It took my forced retirement—giving me the freedom to write, and to reenergize my personal growth. Seeing my own words stare back at me from the screen meant I couldn't hide. I had to face my truth. Being assertive still didn't come easily, but at least I knew the monster's name.

Another monster lurking within me was guilt. When I wrote

about this emotion on social media, friends admonished me to go easy on myself. "Too many mothers are made to feel guilty," they posted. "Motherhood guilt is a turn-off." Adding to the chorus, Mike often reminded me, "You were a great mom." I felt guilty about feeling guilty and struggled to find the balance between holding myself accountable and letting myself off the hook.

But no one can know what lies in another person's heart, what unspoken thoughts swirl in her head. When friends tell me I did everything I could for Matt, they don't know the full picture. Only I knew the dialogue or heard the words I couldn't dredge forward.

In hindsight, it's easy to excuse my failure to speak up more forcefully for the first two years after the onset of Matt's symptoms. The evidence was overwhelming that his changes were simply growing pains. And, I'd read that the brain can temporarily adapt to the presence of a slow-growing tumor, making detection of the anomaly difficult. For Mike, it's easy to excuse his failure to pay attention because he was consumed with managing his newly diagnosed diabetes. Looking back, despite our regrets, I can cut us both some slack.

But that third year...

Mike and I disagree about when on our story timeline he realized something was wrong *that couldn't be fixed by Matt trying harder.* He says he suspected it early in that last pre-diagnosis year. I say he only came on board in the final few months, and that whatever he believed in his heart, if he didn't communicate it in words and actions, how could I have known? Our truths do not align. What we agree on, however, is our shared regret that we hadn't spoken up sooner and louder.

Even the most galvanizing, threatening, bad-ass words from either of us would not have changed the fact of the tumor. But in holding myself accountable, I wonder what could have been.

If standing my ground had shortened Matt's deterioration by a week, a month, a season... If refusing to be silenced had lessened the accumulation of cerebrospinal fluid by a cup, a spoonful, a drop... If I had taken the risk to be disagreeable or disliked...

How much would it have lessened Matt's emotional pain? Softened his journey? Improved his outcome?

Maybe most of the damage had already occurred before that third year of diagnostic darts. Maybe an earlier intervention would not have improved Matthew's abilities. That doesn't change the fact that speaking up was the right thing to do. Holding myself accountable is not about guilt but about integrity.

In twelve-step recovery programs, the fifth step is "Admitting to the higher power, oneself, and another person the wrongs done." What would happen if a recovering person admitted her wrongs, and the receiver of the message responded, "Don't be so hard on yourself?" It would invalidate the recovering person's experience, stymie their growth. Likewise, when I say, "I wish I had spoken up sooner," it's a necessary step in my process of healing, my process of self-forgiveness.

Personal growth is never black-and-white. It is painful and uplifting, demoralizing and redemptive, two steps forward followed by one-and-three-quarters steps backward. Progress is often painfully slow, as it seems to be for me. But inherent in growth is the revelation of our personal truths, and that, I believe, is the path to freedom or enlightenment or fulfilling our purpose in this life.

My process of accepting the best and the worst of myself leads me to two coexisting, contradictory truths. They bring me incredible peace:

As a mother, I whispered when I should have roared.

AND I worked hard at motherhood, facing my fears, and pushing myself to the limits of my endurance. I never gave up on Matthew. I was a good mom, maybe even a great one.

Between suffering physically from my chronic illness, reliving painful memories, and facing hard truths, I decided to return to my Jay Leno look-alike therapist from years before.

"Matt and I had another communication mix-up," I said in one session. The crossed signals brought back the past and worried me about his future.

"It's important to remember to be grateful," Jay said.

I nodded. *Yes. I must remember to be grateful.*

The disconnect between my gut, which told me I felt unheard, and my brain, which told me to be agreeable, was alive and well. I was home before I realized I felt angry. I made excuses for Jay. He knows I'm sad. He doesn't mean to be unsupportive. He's right—I should be grateful.

But that was the old me talking, and I was done living with her regrets.

"I'd like to talk about our last session," I said at my next appointment. I took a deep breath. "I was mad when I left because you sounded dismissive of my sadness." We discussed what happened, Jay apologized, and he agreed to be more sensitive.

I loved the woman who left the office that day. As the door closed behind her, she paused on the stoop to breathe in the fresh air. Diners sipped wine at the sidewalk cafe next door. A young couple laden with boxes approached the post office across the street. A man jogged by, his leashed poodle prancing behind him. Life continued as before, but that woman on the stoop stood taller and had more breadth, more mass, more power than she did an hour before.

One month after my mother, eighty-four, was discharged after open-heart surgery in 2018, I visited my parents. A competent caretaker, my father nonetheless appreciated my support. The hospital was supposed to send a physical therapist for a home visit, but no one had shown up. Dad and I hunched over the phone on a Thursday, listening to a voicemail indicating the PT wouldn't show up until Monday.

"I can't believe this!" I said angrily.

"Karen, it doesn't really matter." Dad splayed his hands out in resignation. "Monday will be fine."

Even with his beloved wife being denied proper care, Dad chose to avoid confrontation, defaulting to his mantra "It doesn't matter." Heaviness settled over me—the sadness of the little girl inside who had never learned to speak up.

I had stopped blaming my parents for who I am. I'd been a resourceful, stable adult for almost forty years and took full responsibly for my actions. Spending time with my parents gave me clarity, though. I judged myself less harshly. I saw how the little girl had grown.

"Dad, it's not okay. That PT was supposed to be here last week."

"Karen, let it go. Monday is fine."

"Not on my watch, Dad."

I picked up the phone and returned the call to Maria at the agency.

"Maria, this is unacceptable."

She made excuses. I asked to speak to someone in charge, but no one was available.

"What are my options, Maria?"

"Well, you could go to another agency."

I dreaded the idea of starting over with a new agency and potentially facing more delays.

"I'll discuss this with my parents and will call you back."

Within ten minutes, Maria called, having miraculously found a PT to come the next day.

Bam! That's how it's done, Dad.

My eighty-five-year-old father was set in his ways and I didn't expect him to change. But I was proud he witnessed my accomplishment. I was also glad he witnessed my next move. Yelling at Maria was a justified option—an elderly person's welfare was put at risk. I could have said, *It's about time you got someone,* and *That PT better show up or I'll be calling the hospital to report your agency!*

But throughout my process of finding and using my voice, I made a conscious decision to retain my essence—to be true to who I was wired to be. I chose not to relinquish my agreeability completely. Broadening my repertoire of reactions enabled me to be assertive when necessary, but I never wanted to lose my soft, gentler side. I love the part of me that can hear a person's story from beginning to end without interrupting. I love that my heart hurts to imagine someone, anyone, in emotional or physical pain, because I never want to become hardened or blind to suffering. I love that I wonder what it's like to walk in another's shoes. I want never to lose empathy. When I'm gone from this earth, I want the wake I leave to be uplifting, not destructive.

"Maria! You're awesome! I really appreciate you making this happen!"

Maria giggled. The PT showed up the next day as promised. I chose to believe that if my parents ran into any more trouble after I left, Maria would go to bat for them more than if I had made a stink.

Some women are born strong. They speak truth to power in their youth, refuse to conform, welcome conflict. Predestined to be activists, they practically come out of the womb holding protest signs. I am awed by their confidence. When an innate warrior fights, she deserves recognition. But it's expected. It's in her nature. And isn't the test of strength defined by tasks that challenge what comes naturally to us?

If I'd held a sign fresh from the womb, it would have read "FRAGILE: HANDLE WITH CARE." By nature and nurture, I wasn't a fighter. Fierceness wasn't in my DNA. When someone like me takes a stand, it is a story meant to be told, a tale of many lessons. My FRAGILE sign had been a means of self-preservation for many years, but it came to feel like a flag of defeat. So I imagined a new sign, one that felt authentic, that honored who I'd been and who I'd evolved to be. It was the message She-bear had conveyed: "WHEN THE WEAK SHOW STRENGTH, THEY ARE STRONGER THAN THE STRONG."

For years, I looked in the mirror, and all I noticed was the jagged crack of fear and self-doubt running through the middle. Shards of glass occasionally splintered off, drawing tears and blood. Now, I have sealed the crack, although it left a scar. The beveled edges are chipped, the antique glass is wavy, the quicksilver is wearing away. But what I notice is character, and I love what I see now.

I love the woman who smiles back.

25

Post-Traumatic Growth

Mike and I take Matt out to dinner at his favorite Mexican restaurant. Matt sits closer to the windows than me, casting his face in shadows, the early evening sunbeams a shimmering halo around him. He looks like a religious icon surrounded by sombreros, clay pottery, and woven baskets.

He tells us about a program he discovered to provide down-payment assistance for first-time home buyers. One of the perks is the program's matching funds, up to $7,500. I wonder how long it will take him to save what sounds like a fortune. But Mike and I both encourage him.

"I'll sign up," Matt says before downing his last sip of Dos Equis XX. "I mean, I already have more than the $7,500 saved, so it should be pretty easy."

Mike and I look at each other over the table. How Matt had saved anything on his low-end salary is beyond my comprehension. From his student loans to his car payments and rent, he is completely self-sufficient. The only way we contribute regularly is to keep him on our family phone plan.

"How did you manage to save that much?" Mike asks.

Matt blushes, running his hands through his hair. "I'm careful with my spending, I guess."

"There are people making three times your salary who couldn't save that much," I say, incredulous.

Matt is accepted into the program, and at the first class, the instructors tell him his credit score, savings record, and accounting practices are so good, he can skip most of the remaining sessions. By the end of the year, his savings total $23,000, and the matching funds will put him over $30,000, a respectable down payment.

In 2019, this child of mine who I feared would be perpetually tied to my apron strings buys the cutest two-bedroom, one-bath bungalow in need of a little—but not too much—TLC. I attend the closing with Matt at his request, a proud mama there purely for moral support. When he has the keys in his hands, we caravan to his house. The inside looks more worn than it had at the open house, but Matt is not deterred.

Standing in the kitchen, we hear skittering in the basement and look at each other in alarm.

"Should we wait for Dad?" I blurt out.

"No," Matt says firmly, like he's the parent and I'm the child. He marches down to the basement, and I follow, crouching behind him. We see no signs of rodents, although a few days after Matt moves in, he calls to say he caught a couple of mice in the basement. That means he bought traps, set them, nailed the perpetrators, and disposed of them. On his own. I shouldn't be surprised, but I'm a slow study.

At thirty-three, this child of mine with a brain tumor asks about my health. He calls or texts Mike and me on our anniversary and to make sure we got home okay in a snowstorm. He takes Mike to a medical procedure when I can't make it, and afterward, gently guides his woozy father into the house. Matt acknowledges he'll be doing more of this—taking care of his parents—as the years progress, and he looks more proud than saddled by that prospect. Mike and I hope to have managed our health and savings enough to never burden our children. But knowing Matt will have our backs gives us both comfort. Matt is the adult child every mom would want. I just happen to be the lucky one who gets him.

One rainy Saturday, Matt comes over and I make us tea. Rain pecks at the kitchen windows while I put two mugs of water in the microwave.

"Mom, did you hear the story about post-traumatic growth on NPR yesterday?"

I hadn't, but I'm intrigued. Matt explains that PTSD—post-traumatic stress disorder—affects many people after a trauma, but if a person experiences growth, they may have PTG—post-traumatic growth.

Raising my eyebrows, I watch him dunk his teabag. I know where he's going with this.

"I think I have that, Mom. I have post-traumatic growth." He wraps his hands around his mug, warming them before taking a sip.

For a moment, I can't reply. I learn much from my son, not

just interesting tidbits of information he gleans from his reading or news or podcasts. With Matt's every struggle and conquest--now as an adult and since he was a newborn screaming in my arms--I learn about myself.

My mind and heart are a tangle of memories, thoughts, emotions. All I can think to say is, "I believe it, Matt. Look how far you've come."

We sip our tea in silence, comfortable with the quiet spaces between spoken words, an introvert characteristic Matt and I have in common. I don't remember when Matt realized he was an introvert. I don't remember if he discovered it on his own or if I opened that door. But we often share resources—books and articles and insights about our similar natures. We learn from each other.

"That PTG concept is fascinating," I say. "Let's look it up." I grab my laptop and move closer to Matt. When I land on an appropriate page, we read silently, shoulder to shoulder.

We learn the term post-traumatic growth was coined in the mid-1990s by two psychologists at the University of North Carolina at Charlotte. Richard G. Tedeschi and Lawrence G. Calhoun defined PTG as "positive change experienced as a result of the struggle with a major life crisis or a traumatic event." *Bingo*.

The theory holds that these positive changes may occur in one or more of five areas: 1) Life or career paths 2) Relationships 3) Inner strength 4) Appreciation for life 5) Spiritual or belief systems.

Two decades of memories stream in front of my eyes. I feel the warmth of Matt's body, smell the licorice tea on his breath.

"What do you think helped you start feeling more positive,

Matt? Because for a while there, when you were in and out of jobs, you had it pretty bumpy."

He looks up at the ceiling, a habit I have, too, when I'm thinking deeply. "I think it's number four." He points to the screen. "Appreciation for life."

I glance at the screen, then back to Matt.

"I think at some point," he says, "I realized I was just happy to be alive."

And at that moment, I become happy. I feel it physically, as if floating but grounded at the same time. My happiness has been in the making for several years, a lightbulb that's flickered on and off. Matt's pronouncement trips the switch that plugs me in.

I've read enough articles, taken enough psychology courses, and been in enough counseling to know that I shouldn't base my mood or emotions on someone else's happiness. For a mother and child, however, it's different. Most mothers will say the one wish they have for their children is happiness. When that wish comes true, we deserve to claim our joy.

I claim mine.

I look at Matt, whose face glows, the radiance coming from within. Noticing the room brightening, I shift my eyes to the window and realize the rain has stopped. The house becomes still. My face warms. A sliver of blue appears on the horizon and sunshine floods the kitchen.

I see that the storm is over.

The author and Matthew today.

Book Club Questions

- Readers know from the title that the mother and son survive a brain tumor. Why do you think the author chose to do this? Does the title spoil the ending?

- What themes made this memoir unique from other worried mother/sick child memoirs?

- How would you characterize Mike (the father)? How did his diabetes affect the trajectory of the story?

- Discuss the helpful and unhelpful messages the author learned from her parents.

- In Chapter 5, the author experiences what she later realizes was postpartum depression. Is it believable that she would not tell her husband about her violent thoughts?

- Discuss the author's binge eating.

- How much do we know about Stephen, the younger brother? Is there a reason the author might have kept his profile in the book to a minimum?

- In Chapter 7, the author asks, "Does blame lie at the feet of the person who doesn't see the problem, or the person who sees the problem and doesn't speak up?" How would you answer that question?

- Is the author's experience of being dismissed by doctors common? Should she have sued Dr. Peterson (the pediatrician)?

- In Chapter 8, the author writes that Matthew's tics "made him odd—which made me the mother of the odd kid." How does society judge parents for their children's behavior and appearance, and vice versa?

- In Chapter 9, the author tells a whiny neighbor, "It sounds like your daughter has destroyed your image of what motherhood should be." In what situations might this happen?

- In Chapter 10, the author writes, "Other moms appeared to take all this in stride—sports, childhood bumps and bruises, the demands of motherhood, even the worrying." Is that true?

- How would an understanding of the concept of neurodiversity have helped the author through Matthew's recovery?

- Discuss She-Bear.

- How might the challenges for people with mild, invisible impairments like Matthew's as an adult compare to the challenges for those with more debilitating and obvious disabilities?

- How is a medical diagnosis or an educational label helpful or hurtful to children? To adults?

- The author refers to her Achilles heel: people-pleasing. What does that concept mean to you? Did you see it at work throughout the book?

- In Chapter 24, the author refers to her son as Matt rather than Matthew. In Chapter 25, she switches from past tense to present tense. Why might she have made these changes?

- This quote appears at the beginning of the book: "If you're acting like a sheep, do not blame the shepherd." How does this relate to the story of Growth?

To schedule a virtual book club visit from the author, please complete the form at https://karendebonis.com/contact/. Or email Karen at contact@karendebonis.com.

For a list of self-reflection questions related to the memoir, go to www.karendebonis.com/reflection.

Acknowledgments

I was not always a writer, but I had a story to tell. So in 1999, when I saw an ad in the Troy NY, paper for a memoir-writing class taught by Marion Roach Smith, I signed up. If Marion had not been so gracious about my bumbling attempts at prose, my story may have remained locked in my heart.

In that class, I met an exquisite writer, Robyn Ringler, who became my friend and later my manuscript editor and mentor for this book. In addition to critiquing my work, Robyn taught me how to create a writer's life and how to lay a path to getting published. I did everything she said and look where it got me.

One of the gifts of my association with Robyn was her introduction to various Facebook writing groups. These beautiful "Binders" became my cheerleaders, my tough-love critics, my virtual friends. They helped make this book possible and continue to inspire me every day.

In one of these groups for published and emerging memoirists, a member asked, "Does anyone want to start a critique group?" That led to my association with Barbie Beaton, Casey Mulligan Walsh, Mimi Zieman, Lindsey DeLoach Jones, Kirsten Ott Palladino, and Eileen Vorbach Collins. If I had to choose the single most influential factor in my writing growth, it would be this bevy of beautiful writers, brilliant editors, and super supporters.

Casey Mulligan Walsh, ambassador of writerly connectivity, invited me to join another critique group where I was warmly welcomed by Judith Fetterley and Marea Gordett, both seasoned and skillful writers.

Finally, before I hit send on my final revisions, I threw a Hail-Mary pass and landed editor Paula Coomer to help polish my words until they shone.

Many other kind, supportive, and inspiring writers joined me on this journey. They are far too many to name, so I won't try, for fear I'll leave someone out. This stems less from people-pleasing than from kindness. How does one thank each drop in an ocean? I haven't figured it out yet, but every day I am grateful the universe threw us together for a swim.

To Kevin Atticks and the Apprentice House Press students: thank you for choosing me, for collaborating, for making my dream come true.

I cannot forget my beta readers. I trusted Ruth Hunter, Judi Reeves, and Liz Shanley with my story, and they helped me dig for my truth. We'll be Prosecco buddies for eternity. And Carol LaCivita, Heather Spitzberg, Laura Massa, Paula Ransbury, and Jill Augustine gave me the final, parting words on my manuscript. I am forever grateful for their careful and thorough reading.

Now, for the ugly-cry acknowledgements:

Mom and Dad–Thank you for giving me the ultimate privilege in life—two parents who loved me unconditionally. And thank you for your blessings on this book. I asked you to read an earlier manuscript in case you were gone before my book was published, and that is what happened. I know you're smiling down on me and see me smiling back.

Michael—My rock, my life partner, my soulmate. I could not have survived this journey of life and writing a book without you by my side. I'll love you forever on this earth and even longer afterward.

Steve—You came into my life when I needed to know I could be a good mom, and your calm, gentle nature showed me that I was indeed a competent and loving mother. You were and are a gift.

Matt—Having you in my life taught me more about humility, perseverance, and pushing past a self-limiting mindset than I ever could have imagined. But mostly, you taught me that I'm strong, that adversity builds character, that you are vastly more capable than I'd imagined. That is a triumph for us both. I am so grateful for you.

About the Author

Retired from a satisfying career in health promotion, Karen DeBonis writes about motherhood, people-pleasing, and personal growth, inspired by the experience of raising her son. Her work has appeared in the *New York Times, HuffPost, Newsweek, Today, Insider, AARP*, and numerous literary journals. Karen relishes her hard-won empty nest in upstate New York with Michael, her husband of forty years.

You can learn more about her at karendebonis.com.

Apprentice House Press
Loyola University Maryland

Apprentice House is the country's only campus-based, student-staffed book publishing company. Directed by professors and industry professionals, it is a nonprofit activity of the Communication Department at Loyola University Maryland.

Using state-of-the-art technology and an experiential learning model of education, Apprentice House publishes books in untraditional ways. This dual responsibility as publishers and educators creates an unprecedented collaborative environment among faculty and students, while teaching tomorrow's editors, designers, and marketers.

Eclectic and provocative, Apprentice House titles intend to entertain as well as spark dialogue on a variety of topics. Financial contributions to sustain the press's work are welcomed. Contributions are tax deductible to the fullest extent allowed by the IRS.

To learn more about Apprentice House books or to obtain submission guidelines, please visit www.apprenticehouse.com.

Apprentice House
Communication Department
Loyola University Maryland
4501 N. Charles Street
Baltimore, MD 21210
410-617-5265
info@apprenticehouse.com
www.apprenticehouse.co

CPSIA information can be obtained
at www.ICGtesting.com
Printed in the USA
BVHW021918210423
662822BV00002B/63

9 781627 204347